Home
Sweet
Home-
school

Home Sweet Home-school

A Survivor's Guide to Giving
Your Kids a Quality Education

SUE MAAKESTAD

Revell
Grand Rapids, Michigan

© 2004 by Sue Maakestad

Published by Fleming H. Revell
a division of Baker Publishing Group
P.O. Box 6287, Grand Rapids, MI 49516-6287
www.bakerbooks.com

Printed in the United States of America

Library of Congress Cataloging-in-Publication Data
Maakestad, Sue
   Home sweet homeschool : a survivor's guide to giving your kids a quality education / Sue Maakestad.
        p.   cm.
   Includes bibliographical references.
   ISBN 0-8007-5930-3 (pbk.)
   1. Home schooling. 2. Faith. I. Title.
LC40.M33 2004
371.04′2—dc22   2004000210

For the fabulous guy who makes me look good, my Mr. Wonderful, boyfriend, main squeeze, and husband of more than thirty years and counting, Chris. Without your sacrificial love, none of us could have learned a thing.

And for my beloved students and awesome blessings: Dina, Mimi, Nathanael, Debbie, Ben, Steve, Joanna, and Daniel. In the course of your schooling, God gave us an education.

Contents

Acknowledgments

God loves me. It doesn't make sense that he should, because he knows the real me. But I thank God for his love and care and mercy and grace upon my life. To him goes all the glory and honor for any semblance of success contained within these pages.

Naturally, without a principal and students there would never have been a homeschool. I'm eternally grateful to my husband and kids for their unbounded patience with me, not only while enduring the trial-and-error process of those long, obscure years, not only in having me write about it, but also—the crowning insult I've added to injury—in having them *help* me write it.

It's a good thing they were brought up to be polite.

My deepest appreciation goes to Bruce Barbour and Vicki Crumpton, whose courage surpassed that of the greatest heroes, because they not only plowed through this material and did worlds to help me improve it, but also sallied forth to convince the world that it should exist. My thanks to Sheila Hagar for graciously allowing me to adapt her original *Oregonian* column "Homeschool and the Average Parent" for use in this book and to all the wonderful, transparent homeschoolers in the trenches who openheartedly shared their stories to bless others. Rest assured: You've made a difference.

Portions of chapters 1 and 2 were previously published as an article ("The Lab Called: Your Brain Is Ready") in *Home Education Magazine* (November/December 2001) and *The California Parent Educator* (February/March 2003). Portions of chapters 3, 7, and 8 were previously published as an article ("Run! Squawk! Flap! Getting Your Homeschool off the Ground") in the *Arizona Families for Home Education Journal* (Fall 2000).

One last heartfelt note of thanks goes to Rosanne LeRoy at the *AFHE Journal,* who first watched over the egg in the incubator and inspired the chicken to take off.

Preface

omeschoolers are unique. As a group, we're somewhat weird and diverse. But that's generally how we like it. We don't do one-size-fits-all answers. We zigzag bikes through traffic jams. Our thinking and approach is often questioned. In response, we simply ask, "You mean there's a box?" But underneath, we're just loving moms and dads who want something better for our kids. And when bucking an entrenched system, it can really be helpful to see the floodlights of success at the end of the long, dark homeschool tunnel.

I wrote this book to offer you this encouragement: We're still here! Alive and mostly well after twenty-four years of homeschooling! We're living proof that homeschooling works for the nobody. Not just for the erudite scholars and fearless leaders of the homeschool world, but for any trembling, educationally challenged, quasi-human, dysfunctional parent who dares to give it a go.

Let's face it: Most of us fit in this category.

We offer you hope—the end of the story. Our eight well-adjusted, independent-minded kids are definitely not the social pariahs the experts and your mother-in-law are telling you homeschooling will produce. On the contrary, our children all attained maturity beyond their years, acquired excellent interpersonal and leadership skills, and currently hold high-paying jobs in the competitive, high-tech real world. And they're all college graduates who love and serve God.

Chris is my husband of thirty years, a tribute to his patience as well as his awesome parenting skills. He was raised a Lutheran and I a Jew. We committed our lives to Christ as teens, giving me added insight and privilege as a messianic Jew. We met and married at a missionary training facility when we were both eighteen and had eight kids by the time we hit thirty. Half of these were home births delivered by Dr. Papa, two of them on a forty-acre plot in northern Arizona without running water or electricity. Two more were born in Mexico. A couple touched down at the hospital. They now range in age from twenty to thirty-one.

Knowing our happy ending, you'd never guess I began my home-teaching career as a high school dropout, quivering down to my toenails at my academic ineptitude. But as I've looked to God as my sufficiency, he's always been there for me. Ultimately I sat in the first college classes of my life—alongside my kids. Now our daughter homeschools our grandsons, ages six and eight. Our two baby granddaughters will soon follow their example. God is a great God!

This isn't a book on selecting curricula or developing unit studies. It doesn't showcase perfect test scores attained by child prodigies and compulsive overachievers. It contains no sparkling rhetoric or theoretical treatise written by pedagogues. It's simply the story of a homeschool family—garden variety, slightly tweaked, and off-base folks who could just as easily live next door to you. Not polished but imperfect—actual, transparent, flawed—people who succeeded in spite of ourselves and because of God's grace.

If he did it for us, we can tell you beyond all doubt he'll do it for you.

In these pages you'll find smoke plumes arising from real daily battles and victories, tips to overcome challenges in scheduling and discipline, creative suggestions on procedure, and timeless truths from God's Word. These tools can be used toward success in anyone's homeschool regardless of style, materials, and kids' personalities. God will help you tailor our ideas and experiences and those of other homeschoolers into the right answer for you, the one that works for your unique homeschool. My prayers go with you as you chart your own course.

—Sue Maakestad

Foreword

I walked into math class on my first day of college. "Can I help you?" asked the instructor.

"Is this Math 122?"

"Yes, it is."

"Oh good," I said, "thank you!" and I proudly sat down. The teacher stared.

"Have . . . you . . . graduated high school?" he asked after a moment of confusion.

"Yyyyesss . . . ," I said with a gentle grin.

"How old are you?"

"Fifteen," I said, not bothering to tell him that my birthday was only last week.

He asked how that was possible, and I explained I'd been homeschooled. I could tell it made a favorable impression on him. I think up until that moment he thought I was a lost little girl looking for her mother.

I'll admit I was nervous at first. New school, weird people, everybody older than me. But all those homeschool years paid off. Despite my age I felt prepared. Within a few weeks, I'd made lots of friends and felt right at home.

It was fun telling people that my mom homeschooled all eight of us. Of course, I was often obliged to produce family pictures to verify my story. The instructors enjoyed that though, and it made me feel special. Being taught at home *was* special, and we've had some good times.

Mama always had us read aloud so she could hear us while she did the dishes. Three or four of us reading different lessons simultaneously at our lesson stations got pretty interesting. And noisy. And confusing. So two kids would stop reading and act out the story of the third, till the giggles gave us away.

"Are we doing our lessons?" Mom would say. "Daniel, I can't hear you!"

In later years, Mama sometimes left for the store, thinking her younger angels were all doing lessons under the care of the older ones. The door closed. At first there was perfect silence. We'd all look at each other.

I don't know how it began, but the inevitable pillow fight always kept us running from one end of the house to the other, seeking refuge by doing flying leaps—with the appropriate Superman pose—onto our parents' big queen-size bed. Then we'd rush to clean everything up and do a little schoolwork before Mama got back to ask what we'd done while she was gone.

Now, don't get me wrong: Homeschool wasn't always a bed of roses. I hated geography and history because I got really stressed out over stuff I didn't understand, but I eventually got through all that. I never got really excited about reading either, because many of the schoolbooks were really boring. But when I got a bit older, I started reading the *Cooper Kids Adventures* by Frank Peretti and found I couldn't put them down. Now I love to read, and I order books left and right off the Internet, usually during breaks at work, where I use the Web to configure phone systems on the other side of the world.

Somehow we all survived and turned out okay, and I thank God for my parents' vision to see that their children got the education they needed to make it on their own.

Now I know I can look at life and say, "I'm ready. Bring it on!"

—Joanna Maakestad

As the oldest of the eight kids, I had the honor of being the first guinea pig in line for our great excursion called homeschool. All in all, it was a positive journey, and my recollections of it are mostly pleasant. My fondest memories are of finishing school early enough to be rewarded with an outing to the park or the library.

And I always eagerly looked forward to summer vacation.

All the neighbor kids used to tell me how lucky I was to be homeschooled. At the time I responded with a puzzled look on my face and wondered, *Why?* But looking back, I see all the advantages we had, and so I've chosen to homeschool my own children.

In the back of my mind, I always knew this was what I wanted for my kids. But after seeing firsthand the great amount of sacrifice required for the task, I really didn't want to be the one to undertake it. Maybe I could hire somebody . . . ?

As the time approached, I made a deal with God. If he wanted me to homeschool my kids, he'd have to supply the money or the resources. It seemed my only logical way out.

Two weeks after discussing the matter with God, I received a box in the mail from my aunt on the East Coast with whom I hadn't spoken in ages. In it were all her kids' old homeschool curricula and texts. Realizing this was confirmation from the Lord, I launched my own career in home education. If I survive, you may someday be reading a book by me.

But in the meantime, I'll join the throngs of other families out there who day by day invest their time and energy in one of the most meaningful, rewarding pursuits parents can undertake for their children's future.

—Dina R. Gastelum

Light in the
Black Hole

Who Knew God Knew?

Two of the four young Mexican ladies held toddlers on their laps. One nursed her baby while she studied along in my kitchen in Monterrey. The card I held up showed a hand, fingers pointed down, with dark outlines around the middle three to represent the letter *m*.

"Mano—mmm," the girls said, naming the picture in Spanish and its initial letter sound.

The new converts, excited about reading their Bibles, were learning to read and write Spanish for the first time in their lives. I was proud to be their tutor.

It was spring 1968 in Nuevo León, Mexico. I was fourteen.

Two lovely young blondes ages one and two sat beside me on the office couch. I held up a card showing an apple alongside the letter *a*.

"Apple—ă," chorused my girls, giving the appropriate short vowel sound.

I was excited about teaching my kids their letters and amazed at their terrific absorbency at such an early age.

It was fall 1975 in Phoenix, Arizona. I was twenty-one.

A handsome young man in a black cap and gown stood beside me in my living room. I held up his high school diploma and shook his hand. I gave him a hug and congratulated myself on not getting weepy at this, our last homeschool graduation. Our previous seven graduates-turned-college-students joined him, carrying another diploma for me. I had recently finished the same correspondence high school. It read:

CERTIFICATE OF APPRECIATION

Awarded to Susan Abigail Maakestad
For all the years of your life that you've dedicated
to our education while postponing your own.
We're very proud of you as you graduate
and thank you for your love and dedication.
Love, the Kids

It was signed by each of my erstwhile students, as was the accompanying gift of a stuffed cloth apple. They each hugged me in turn. I got weepy.

It was summer 1998 in Tucson, Arizona. I was forty-five.

Have you ever felt as if you've been set up?

I should have seen the sucker punch coming way back on that lovely spring afternoon in Monterrey. Who knew that God planned to bring me back from Mexico to Phoenix to meet and marry the most wonderful guy on earth? Who knew God knew we'd have eight great kids? Who knew God knew we'd decide to homeschool them even before the first was born? Who knew that God planned to give us twenty-four wonderful homeschooling years, not just for our own benefit, but in order to encourage many others? Who knew that God would put it in our kids' hearts to homeschool our grandkids?

God's so smart. He knows that if he told us this kind of stuff up front, we'd certainly opt out early. But he also knows that if we just stick with him and do what he sets before us because we know it's a rough job but somebody's gotta do it—and because we know he's able even if we aren't—he'll always pull off great things in spite of us.

And we know if God did it for our family, he can do it for virtually anybody.

We put our hand to the homeschool plow during the Dark Ages, the seventies, when this form of education was perceived as illegal, deficient, and in all other possible ways offensive. Nobody was in our corner. No support groups. No Homeschool Legal Defense Association (HSLDA). No enlightenment—but plenty of dragons. Every other week we'd read of another homeschool family who had their kids legislated away from them on charges of "academic child abuse."

Absolutely no decent alternative curricula were available. "Christian" curricula were nothing more than watery academics with Bible verses slapped onto the page at intervals to justify their claim to Christianity. No wonder national magazine covers blasted home education as academically deficient. At that time, many of their claims were way beyond justifiable. But at the same time, I remember our horror at reading newspaper stories decrying the lack of education among military recruits. At eighteen years old, most of these traditional high school grads were unable to read, write, or compute math at anything more than a third-grade level. Naturally, nobody made the same "academically deficient" claim against the public schools, regardless of its veracity. Many of these deficiencies are still evident today.

Recently I arrived at the elementary school where I volunteered as a literacy tutor and found that one of my third graders had been moved to the special ed reading class.

"Lawrence doesn't need a special ed reading class," I told the supervisor. "He's been effortlessly reading three pages a day for me."

I hunted down the special ed teacher and found Lawrence with three other kids, learning what sound the letter *o* makes. The instructor was a bit shocked to discover that Lawrence was pulling the wool over her eyes and had simply chosen to be a lazy reader that day. If nobody had blown the whistle on him, he would probably have been happy to stay there and underachieve indefinitely.

Conversely, several years ago I had the privilege of teaching a thirty-year-old mom to read for the first time in her life. Having attended traditional schools, she had been kicked from one grade to the next and finally awarded a high school diploma in spite of her inability to read.

But homeschooling was academic child abuse. Hey, what did we know?

Back then we were on our own in the black hole. No groups existed to organize kids from several families into homeschool athletic teams or bands or field-trip groups. I guess we would have done so ourselves had there been anyone else around to organize. But homeschoolers were frowned upon as out-there hippies and rebels. So if there were any others, they were most likely hiding out somewhere on the backside of the desert, just as we were.

It was us and nobody. Except God.

So who else did we need? We knew God had called us to do this, so we dug in our teeth and our toenails and committed to it, and he blessed it in spite of us. And after all, isn't that the usual way we receive blessings? I mean, when's the last time you were blessed because of how wonderful you are? I daresay it was because of how wonderful and benevolent God is. He's a good

Count Your Blessings!

Don't miss opportunities for networking with other homeschoolers:

- Area conventions and curriculum fairs
- Joint field trips, dramas, and recitals
- Co-ops: afternoon language, drama, music, dance, art, and computer classes
- Mom's day off: homeschooling and baby-sitting rotation groups
- Joint bands and athletic teams
- Internet sharing and Q&A (www.homeschool zone.com)
- After-hours snack-and-study group rotations
- Joint swimming, library, picnic, and shopping afternoons
- Combined year-end promotion and graduation parties
- Weekend sleepovers, campouts, and summer activities
- Morning coffee, evening potluck, and church fellowship

Above all: Seek out your local support group! (www.kingsharvest.com/Support.html)

Dad. He knows how to smile and say, "Yes, dear, I'm so proud of you," and hug us with one great big hand while cleaning up our mess with the other.

Thank God for God.

A Is for Ape

Schooling our kids in the Dark Ages had its interesting moments. In the seventies, word recognition was a reading system that held an unchallenged educational dictatorship. Phonics, on the other hand, was regarded as methodology non grata, as useful and desirable as a bad trip on LSD.

Having both heartily embraced phonics growing up as literate children, and now as homeschooling adults, my husband and I were used to driving around with the three-year-old spouting off from the back seat at regular intervals as road signs slid by his window.

"St-op—STOP? Sp-ee-d li-m-it—SPEED LIMIT."

"Betcha can't read this one," taunted a sibling.

"Yi-el-d . . . Mama, what's yi-eld? . . . yelled?"

So much for the consistencies of the English language.

I held a toddler on my lap for immunizations at the county health clinic one day while two of the older kids took eye exams in the next room. A nurse with a knit brow materialized at the exam room door.

"I think I need an interpreter or something," she said.

"Having trouble?" quipped the nurse injecting the baby.

"Yeah. I don't get what this kid is saying. Can you come, please?" she asked me.

As I entered, four-year-old Dina shot a *what's-this-woman's-problem?* glance at me, aimed at the nurse's back.

24

"Okay, dear, now, read the eye chart for Mom. This line down here."

"Fff, zzz, ŏ, mmm, ă, rrr, jjj, nnn. . . ."

"Okay, okay, that's good. . . . Mom?"

"Yep, she read it for you. It's all correct."

"She did?"

"Yes. She read it phonetically."

"Really," said the nurse. "Then what happened to *A* is for apple?"

"Oh, no," said Dina. "Only ă can be for apple, because the ă has two consonants after it so it stays short. Ā can be for ape, though," she offered. "That word has a long vowel sound."

"Why can't she just tell me the letter names?" asked the nurse.

"Don't muddy the waters," I said. "They learn letter names after letter sounds. And the short vowel sounds come first. Names come with the long vowel sounds later. Till then, they may sing their ABCs, but from the page they must read off letter sounds."

"But, why?"

"Why is cuz Mama says so," my daughter chirped.

Such a brilliant child.

Certainly most homeschoolers of the new millennium wouldn't want to use these unorthodox methods to teach reading, as well they shouldn't. We only had Maakestad phonics. We didn't have the benefit of educational software featuring word games or sentence munchers back then. In fact, we didn't have the benefit of a computer then. To us a Tandy Commodore keyboard hooked up to a TV was cutting-edge technology.

But we had grace. And God's grace is always beyond sufficient.

Somehow our kids not only learned to read but have joined their parents in their never-ending mission: to seek out functionally illiterate adults in America and educate them. In the far reaches of the nation somewhere, this very moment, a Maakestad is undoubtedly editing something, whether invited to or not. They're defenders of the English language.

I had a call from my eldest son the other day. After being stationed in Korea for a whole ten days, he was cruising the local marketplace, cell phone in hand, with a bunch of fellow U.S. soldiers for whom he was the acting interpreter. I told him I thought that was admirable, given the fact that he'd never studied Korean.

"What in the world are you telling these people?" I said. "How do you know you're not telling them their deodorant doesn't work?"

"Mom," he said. "Don't worry. I'm picking up this language really fast."

Yeah, right. Just fast enough to get into trouble, no doubt. But at least he's not afraid to try, and that's something I attribute to homeschooling as well. After bucking the incumbent system and winning, you and your offspring come away with a strong *why not?* outlook on life. This is sometimes a good thing. And at other times . . . well . . . what my kids lack in wisdom they make up for in spunk.

Phone Calls from the Edge

One of my married daughters, Dina, the eldest, called the other day in a moment of homeschool desperation. Ever since her older son, Daniel, figured out that those funky-looking letters made words, he has devoured books by the trainload. He could find excitement in a mausoleum if he were to discover a book there.

Josh, two years younger, is the quintessential dreamer. In his case, paying attention long enough to read a three-letter word—let alone a complete sentence—would bring a standing ovation from the sidelines.

"Mom! I just can't do this," Dina said.

"Really? That's *great!*" I said. "You're in a fabulous position. Because when we reach the end of ourselves, we're ready to give it to God and see him move."

"But I just don't have that kind of patience."

"Well, you've come to the right place: Tribulation worketh patience. And when it comes to tribulation, teaching a kid to read can be right up there with the transitional phase of labor."

"Oh, please, don't say that," said Dina, who'd recently had a particularly trying labor with the boys' baby sister.

"No, no, no. I don't mean in *that* way. I mean it's like transition because it's the hardest part, but it also means two very positive things: It means you're almost done, and it means it's never going to be this hard again. And, hey, isn't it worth all that?"

"I dunno. Is it?"

"Was Julia worth all that?"

"Well, of course! I mean, is *this* worth all that?"

"It is."

That's not the response I'd have given at the beginning of my homeschool career. Patience was not my forte then and still isn't. Patience is an ongoing and excruciating process for me, right up there with the diet-and-weight-loss battle. Erma Bombeck said she was proud to report she'd lost five hundred pounds by dieting, five pounds at a time. Only problem—they were the same five pounds. I can *so* relate to that! And this is after I've consumed dehydrated water and rice cakes almost exclusively for a six-month period.

Knowing all this about myself, I burst into fits of uncontrollable laughter when I hear someone say, "Oh, my! You must have *so* much patience!" This is generally the knee-jerk reaction from some naive soul who's just met us and learned we have eight kids. After regaining sufficient oxygen, we explain to them that patience isn't a function of having many kids; on the contrary, *lack* of patience is. They laugh politely and never seem quite convinced.

Then again, they don't have eight kids.

The truth is that God gave us eight kids because he believed we could handle it, although exactly why he thought so remains a mystery to me. It's one of the many questions I mean to ask him when I finally see him face-to-face.

On the other hand, a dear friend of mine was blessed with a newborn when her youngest was fourteen, and I know for a fact that I couldn't handle that—not with the finish line of the parenting race in sight. But God knows that about me. He also knew my friend could be trusted with that blessing. And as I watch her raise her daughter, I see how she's been able to take the sum of all knowledge and wisdom she's gleaned during her parenting career and do a perfectly magnificent job with her new child. We've all said those sadder-but-wiser parenting words, "If I'd only known then what I know now . . ." But we never quite go as far as saying we'd like another kid to try it out on, huh? Here are some folks who have had the insight and patience born of past years of parenting to do just that. And that's because God knows they're able to handle it.

Just like he knew eight was our number. All parents have their own number. In some cases, that number is one, because that one kid makes up for all eight of someone else's. But God has promised never to give us more than we can bear. The Bible says that along with the temptation (trial, hassle, seemingly insurmountable circumstance), he supplies the way of escape (1 Cor. 10:13). As we work through all the stuff we don't think we can handle—just when we think we're on the verge of a nervous breakdown and right before it occurs—he gives us the patience to deal with it and/or them.

Thank God children don't arrive in litters! It took all of ours born one by one—with breathing time in between—to get us to the place where handling them seemed like a viable option this side of heaven. This was only by God's enabling. The same held true for homeschooling, where his overwhelming grace prevailed in our monumental weakness.

What, Me Teach?

We discovered in the course of our career a basic tenet of homeschooling: The more kids you have in one place, the fewer brain cells are available among them. At four or five students, you find a looser grip on reality. At six you experience mild delirium. At eight, you've achieved the destructive power of a Sherman tank driven by a Saint Bernard. Just ask me how I know.

Let's look at our place on an average school day:

The cat's caught a mouse. Two of my child prodigies are dutifully dissecting it, staining it, and preparing a slide to put under the microscope for science class. Another two do their math in the kitchen, where they pour red fruit juice from my gallon pitcher into a two-cup measure to discover how many gallons fit into a pint. The toddler finger-paints the white kitchen tile with the overflow.

So much for art class.

I cradle the nursing baby in one arm and hold up animal picture cards in the other for the two-year-old to identify. As he tries to decide between the names of both the animals he knows this card contains, I hold my breath and raise an encouraging eyebrow.

In a barely audible whisper he proclaims, "Rhi . . . potonus."

"Say it louder," I prod, hoping for a final decision.

He scrunches his eyes shut, wrinkles his nose, and clenches his fists.

In a thin, high-pitched voice he squeaks, *"Rhipotonus!"*

There's a commotion at the back door. The dog drags himself up the steps, having been on the wrong side of a considerable disagreement. Today's field trip is to a veterinary office.

I pile the kids and the dog into the car. Now I notice the puddle of soft vulcanized rubber under the wheel rim. The tire passed away last night and has awaited me with expectant glee ever since. The lug nuts haven't been budged since the Revolutionary War. This provides relevant material for history class. I empty two cans of Liquid Wrench over them while the kids call out tearful reminders from the interior that Fido may expire any second.

Days like these make me wonder if I can muster enough collective brain cells and achieve a sufficient level of peace amid the pandemonium to conduct some sort of teaching, let alone impart pedagogical wisdom. My married daughter came over the other day to tap into what she thought was left of it.

"Hi, Mom. Hey, I just came over to roast some chilies. While I'm doing that, can you teach me real quick how to homeschool the kids?"

Oh, yeah, right, sure. No sweat!

What, me homeschool? But then I consider the alternatives. The media make heroes of spoiled kids who have no respect for adults. Then we expect kids who idolize these heroes to be well behaved in classrooms. When, as a natural result, classroom discipline fails, they're medicated with Ritalin. Certainly our faith isn't at the top of the teacher's list if she gets to teach them anything at all in the time remaining.

Sure makes the chaos of my homeschool day look preferable.

Yeah, but Will It Work?

Homeschool works for all those willing to dig in, partner with God, and stick to their guns. If you know that God's there for you—if you're not afraid to jump a few hurdles and kill a few giants—you and he can do it together.

How can we be so sure?

Schooled at home from before birth, our own kids never attended a formal school until they entered college at age fourteen or fifteen. Now they're gainfully employed graduates. More than able to exist in the cold, cruel, real world of hard knocks, they've all landed high-tech, high-paying jobs in a competitive market, most of them in people-related areas.

Humor me for a moment while I introduce them.

Where Are the Maakestad Kids Now?

Dina Maakestad Gastelum entered Pima Community College (PCC) at the age of fifteen. She graduated with a small-business computer specialist degree and subsequently worked for Apple Computers. She is now the stay-at-home mom of Daniel, eight, and Joshua, six, whom she is homeschooling, and their baby sister, Julia Faith, eighteen months. She and her husband, John, lead a Bible study group in their home and are active in music and drama ministries. Dina sings with a Christian

31

country and western band and offers cooking classes in her home for young ladies at church. She's thirty-one.

Naomi Maakestad entered PCC at fifteen, graduated with a premed degree, and transferred to the University of Arizona, where she completed her BSN and became a registered nurse. By age nineteen Naomi was doing off-the-cuff Spanish translations for patients in the ER where she worked while going to school, and at twenty-four she paid her own way to Sierra Leone, West Africa, where she treated thousands of people and saw many miraculous healings during two weeks with a medical mission team. She was active in drama ministries before becoming a travel nurse. She now serves in emergency rooms around the U.S. and abroad. She's thirty.

Nathanael Maakestad entered PCC at fifteen and graduated with two degrees: one in electronics and another in computer technology. A semiconductor engineer who built chipboards to drive military tanks and helicopters, he was active in technical and children's church ministries before enlisting in the army, where he's now completing a bachelor's program as a microwave communications expert and is training to be a helicopter pilot. He discovered at age twenty-one that he adored ice-skating. Jumping into classes alongside four- to ten-year-olds without a second thought, he went on to win awards at competitive events. He's twenty-eight.

Debbie Maakestad Orr entered PCC at fifteen and graduated with a computer specialist degree. She worked as a phone support technician for Microsoft before she married. She's now a stay-at-home wife and mom who plans to homeschool her daughter, Dianna Ruth, age one. Having achieved the dream of making her own elaborate wedding dress, Debbie also upholsters and does custom sewing upon request. Deb and her husband, Paul, participate in several children's ministries and lead a Bible study on Davis Monthan Air Force Base. She's twenty-six.

Ben Maakestad entered PCC at fourteen and transferred to the University of Arizona, where he completed a degree in mechanical engineering. He moved to Detroit upon graduation to work as a design engineer for the auto industry. Before he left he was our church's Saturday drama-and-music-night pyrotechnic special-effects guy. As his last church project in town, he designed and operated an award-winning float for the Tucson Rodeo Parade that carried a six-foot cowboy roping a five-foot smoke-breathing devil. Ben now lives and works in Ohio as a design engineer for Ford/Visteon and is active in outreach with area churches. He's twenty-five.

Steve Maakestad entered PCC at fifteen and completed two degrees and a certificate in computer technology and networking. At nineteen, while still a student there, he served as the college's computer lab supervisor and network technician. The college subsequently employed him as permanent staff in these capacities. He remains at work there today. While achieving professional certifications on the side, he also serviced the church's computer network, most of which he built singlehandedly. You'd never know. When I ask this guy what to do with my home computer because it's blanking out on me, he gives me his all-purpose answer: "Kick it!" For this I sent him to college? Steve is also active in technical and drama ministry. He and his new wife, Melissa, both serve in children's church. He's twenty-three.

Joanna Maakestad entered PCC at fifteen and graduated with a computer specialist degree. At twenty she took a job configuring and servicing business phone systems worldwide via the Internet for firms that include Honeywell and America West Airlines. By then she had designed and helped build several *Sesame Street*–quality puppets and performed with international Christian puppetry teams. She and her two best friends learned sign language in response to a need at church and were inspired to form Signs and Wonders, a group that interprets popular Christian songs through sign language and choreography. She's also active in children's ministries and puppet outreach teams and teaches puppetry at church. She's twenty-two.

Daniel Maakestad entered PCC at fifteen and completed a computer software degree. At eighteen, he was entrusted with maintenance and intercampus delivery of fleet vehicles at the college. Then he moved to Scottsdale, Arizona, to study at a Cordon Bleu culinary institute in pursuit of his dream to become a master chef. He's been active in video, lighting, and tech support ministries; children's ministries; drama ministries; and puppet outreach teams. He's twenty.

This is not mere parental bragging. Okay, well, yeah, it's that too. But more important, it's a track record showing the fruits of God's grace upon our homeschooling labors and what *your* efforts in his grace can produce as well: educated, well-adjusted, God-loving, and mostly sane kids who have emerged from the other end of the homeschool experience as independent thinkers and productive citizens.

"All big men are dreamers," said Woodrow Wilson. "They see things in the soft haze of a spring day or in the red fire of a long winter's evening. Some of us let these great dreams die, but others nourish and protect them; nursing them through the bad days till they bring them to the sunshine and light which comes always to those who sincerely hope that their dreams will come true."[1]

Such is the power of hope. Now imagine what could happen with the power of prayer.

Imagine the possibilities for your own crew when you consider the fact that we ourselves were—and still are—a bunch of real, live, imperfect, flawed, clueless people who somehow by God's grace blundered through to home-education success. No posturing, no preparation, no golden curricula, and very few brains. And God was our only ally.

But, hey, he's the guy with the big guns. Never doubt that he'll do it for you too.

Lifesavers

(Mmm . . . Make Mine Cherry!)

1. When I find myself drowning in the daily craziness of running a homeschool household, I cry out to God, and he always throws me a lifesaver. Deep in the recesses of my mind—buried a little deeper some days than others—are many gems from his Word that he brings to my remembrance just in time. As you seek him daily and dive into his love letter to you (the Bible), you'll wrap up several rolls of these goodies, and God will pop 'em out as needed in your homeschool career. The first ones out of the wrapper are a twofer:

Thy word have I hid in mine heart, that I might not sin against thee.

Psalm 119:11 KJV

Thy word is a lamp unto my feet, and a light unto my path.

Psalm 119:105 KJV

2. Never doubt that if God put it into your heart to homeschool, he's already put time and effort into seeing that you're equipped for the job. Homeschooling is as much a calling as preaching. It's a God-given ministry. And it's not a surprise to him that you're homeschooling. He planned it from way back when:

> Then the word of the Lord came to me saying:
> Before I formed you in the womb I knew you;
> Before you were born I sanctified you;
> I ordained you a prophet to the nations.

Jeremiah 1:4–5

For I know the thoughts that I think toward you, says the LORD, thoughts of peace and not of evil, to give you a future and a hope.

Jeremiah 29:11

3. We know one thing for certain: If we could do this homeschool thing by the grace of God, then anybody can do it. Remember: Nothing ventured, nothing gained. The Jordan didn't part till the priests got their feet wet.

> Sow your seed in the morning,
>   and at evening let not your hands be idle,
> for you do not know which will succeed,
>   whether this or that,
>   or whether both will do equally well.

Ecclesiastes 11:6 NIV

4. If you feel deficient and powerless like we did starting out (and at many times thereafter), then rejoice! You're in a fabulous place for God to show his power.

And He said to me, *"My grace is sufficient for you, for My strength is made perfect in weakness."* Therefore most gladly I will rather boast in my infirmities, that the power of Christ may rest upon me. Therefore I take pleasure in infirmities, in reproaches, in needs, in persecutions, in distresses, for Christ's sake. For when I am weak, then I am strong.

2 Corinthians 12:9–10, emphasis added

"We Have Met the Enemy and He Is Us"

Your Ticket to Ride

I stir my coffee with a fork handle.

Not every morning, just mornings like this when finding a spoon is an insurmountable task. But wait! What pitter-patter of little feet do I hear at this ungodly hour?

Oh, yeah, it's the thundering herd. Wait a minute. Wasn't I their mom or something? "Mama!"

"Oh, hey, it must be Saturday, huh? You guys would never be up this early on a school day."

"I was on the computer first, and Debbie's shoving her way in."

"I'm not shoving. I called it first."

"No, I called it first."

"Well, *I* called it last night."

"Hey, I'm calling you both: Earth to kids! Have you hugged your room today?"

"I hugged my pillow."

"Nice try. Now go hug your bed and get a grip on your room."

"Mommmm! That's not fair. How can you be so awake so early?"

"Look who's talking."

Ding! End round one. Winner: Mom.

Homeschooling is like a trip to Six Flags. First you take a look at the glitzy advertising brochure. The people suspended upside down by their earlobes look elated. Twenty-eight dollars seems a trivial price to pay for the promise of spectacular speed, corkscrew turns, G-forces plastering your lips onto your cheeks, and eyelashes fusing with hair follicles on the back of your head. You decide to go.

Falling in line, you notice the ride looks more ominous in 3-D. Signs warn, "This ride isn't advisable for people with bad hearts, hypertension, weak intestinal constitutions, loose dentures, morning sickness, or ingrown toenails. Please secure all necklaces, bracelets, earrings, ears, hair, fingernails, eyebrows, fingers, and all articles of clothing not directly contacting human epidermis. Said epidermis must be free of chapped lips and paper cuts. Method of securing these items is left up to the individual. Thank you. The Management."

The warnings grow more serious as you approach the point of no return. Your initial amusement gives way to healthy respect. Then panic. Your mouth goes dry as the vehicle of death looms before you. You swallow hard, tough it out, and board the ride. The executioners strap you in. You close your eyes and scream your guts out. Halfway through you hazard a peek with half an eyeball, and the swirling surroundings prove the truth that your brain wants to reject: This is it. You're in a wormhole. You're going toward the bright light.

Suddenly the churning in your gut abates. Your brain stops gyrating. The ride slows and finally stops. You're dumped out alive and well on terra firma. Immediately you're invincible.

"Wanna go again?" you challenge your companions.

Starry-eyed newcomers approach homeschooling with even less warning. Our ticket-booth high quickly subsides as we board the vehicle and the upward climb begins. By the time we kind of sort of think we maybe realize what lies ahead, we're halfway down the first high-speed plummet, and the momentum picks up from there.

Time to refer to our manual: *Mother Murphy's Laws for Homeschoolers.*

Mother Murphy's Law #1: Nobody wants your job, but everyone thinks they can do it better than you.

Albert Einstein said, "Great spirits have always encountered violent opposition from mediocre minds."[1] The greatest bulk of unsolicited advice you will encounter arrives with the birth of your first child and exponentially increases with your decision to homeschool.

Arm yourself: Be proud to be the only weirdo. Don't care what people think of you. Don't care if your mother-in-law says you're sapping the above-average brains of her erudite grandchildren through your amateurish efforts at teaching. Don't care that the car is broken-down again and so the best you can manage for your kids' field trip is a couple of laps around the backyard to find grasshoppers and topsoil with the dog. Don't care if your friends are sipping coffee and nibbling crumpets at midmorning brunch and clucking their tongues over poor you—while you're home, still in your pj's at noon, trying to figure out why Train A and Train B had to leave the station going opposite directions.

Know Your Enemy

Awe is the bug-eyed, open-mouthed *wow!* state of wonder that we achieve when we know who we are and who God is and realize he loves us anyway.

David achieved this state in Psalm 8:3–6:

> When I consider Your heavens, the work of Your fingers,
> The moon and the stars, which You have ordained,
> What is man that You are mindful of him,
> And the son of man that You visit him?
> For You have made him a little lower than the angels,
> And You have crowned him with glory and honor.
> You have made him to have dominion over the works
>   of Your hands;
> You have put all things under his feet.

Many of you are wasting a whole lot of valuable time worrying about *you*.

You feel assaulted, unworthy, and in all other ways pathetic. Why? Because you're a stay-at-home mom? Because you don't have a Ph.D.? You have doubts about whether you can do the homeschool thing? Well, let me take a moment to set your mind at ease.

Of course you can't! Only Jesus can. Why is this any different from anything else?

What's the matter? You thought God wasn't prepared for your inadequacies? That's like God being shocked that Adam and Eve sinned. You'd be surprised how many people think God panicked, killed that animal, and threw clothes on them as a spur-of-the-moment recovery move. Can't you just picture him collapsing on top of the carcass, wiping the sweat from his brow, and pulling himself together? No, this wasn't a surprise to God. He knows everything. We're the clueless ones.

Not only is he omniscient, but he's also omnipotent and omnipresent. That means he's always there for us, and nothing is impossible with God.

So why are we always sweating the small stuff? Oh sure, we can believe all the big stuff—that Jesus came and died for us to totally wipe our sins away and make us children of God who can approach the throne of grace and ask him for whatever we need without being fried by a lightning bolt. That's simple. But somehow we don't really believe we can ask for *anything* we need. Because we can't believe him for the little things—like wisdom to help us homeschool.

Is this too big for God? A bit too much for him? A tad beyond his scope?

I don't think so. It's not really about whether we think he can handle it. It's about whether we think *we* can handle it. Now, stop for a moment: Why do we think we're the ones handling it? Because we forget that we can only do this homeschooling thing because he can. We forget he's God and we're us.

We forget who we are. We forget who he is. We lose the awe.

So you lack knowledge. God *knows* that you don't know. But remember, he used those clueless fishermen in spite of the overwhelming odds against them. Acts 4:13–14 tells us about Peter and John's defense before the Sanhedrin after they were arrested for healing the lame man at the Gate Beautiful and gives the response of the four high priests: "Now when they saw the boldness of Peter and John, and perceived that they were uneducated and untrained men, they marveled. And they realized that they had been with Jesus. And seeing the man who had been healed standing with them, they could say nothing against it." In other words, God was these guys' credentials, because it obviously wasn't them pulling it off.

Now, I'm not a card-carrying teacher. Deep down I know who I really am, just as you do. I'm just Mom. Just diaper-changing, dish-washing, get-the-door-for-the-UPS-guy-in-my-grungies-and-no-makeup, and get-the-phone-with-the-kids-screaming-their-heads-off-in-the-background Mom. I pulled the dog out of the overturned trash can by his tail, wiped peanut butter off the light bill before I could pay it, and nursed sick parakeets back to dubious states of health.

On the side I moonlighted, teaching my kids lessons I had never learned myself—because Mom was a high school dropout. Not a deliberate move, no. It was a result of leaving for Mexico to do missionary work with my parents at the age of thirteen. But the end result was the same: I never went back. So however little you think you know, you certainly know a whole lot more starting out than I did.

That should give you barrels of hope. After all, Christians are just sinners saved by grace. And homeschoolers are just moms who pray for grace and let God do the rest. That's exactly what I did. I *knew* I'd never pull it off alone; it *had* to be God. Usually it had to be God, me, and the whole team. I had to call for backup plenty of times. When the kids got into high school and were doing algebra beyond what I had learned (not a far stretch), it was time for Papa the draftsman math guru to take the wheel. When he was busy, there was always Auntie Beth the math whiz. Later, Mom herself employed the college algebra tutorial services of her son Ben. So why are you battling with doubt? If you doubt yourself, great! Join the club.

I have a lifetime, ironclad, titanium-plated membership.

But I also know in whom I have believed, and I know that I'm able because he is able. As parents, we're partners with God in our greatest earthly endeavor—raising kids. Now, I ask you seriously: Do you think you can parent without God? Do you think you can live a Christian life without God? Do you think you can think your next thought without God? Do you think you can take your next breath without God? Good. I didn't think so.

So quit thinking you have to do the homeschool thing yourself, and there won't be a problem.

But how will you know what to teach your kids? How will you know what to do? How will you know what to say? Easy. The same way a bunch of illiterate fishermen wound up speaking with authority before princes and kings. Read some of Peter's sermons in the first few chapters of Acts. He's hardly recognizable when you remember he was quivering in his sandals just a few pages back in the judgment hall. That's why Jesus told these folks not to go anywhere till they had the power of the Holy Spirit on their side (Acts 1:4–8).

Now, remember who these guys were. They caught fish for a living. Not too impressive. You'd think God would choose decorated nobility in high places who had it all together and didn't smell like sushi.

But . . . why would he? He knew power and prestige weren't important. He knew it wasn't about them but about his power working through them. He knew they could do it, because he'd do it through them. And just as God gave the apostles words to speak by his Spirit when they were needed, he'll do the same for you. That's what I call living by faith.

Why do we have faith in every other area except where we feel destiny hinges on our own abilities?

What Do You Expect?

Why is this about you? Aren't you homeschooling because God wants you to? I'd assume that's so. In that case, you've gone before him for help, putting your homeschooling in his hands. Is God a failure? Is anything too hard for the Lord?

It's not a trick question. It's a rhetorical question. Like when we ask our kids, "Did you wash your hands?" It's not as if you expect the answer to be yes.

Every now and then we all have bad homeschool days. Okay, maybe it's a bad week. Or even a month. But be

Navigating the System

Help is at your fingertips! Inform yourself. Investigate for your area:

Homeschool laws and rights (www.hslda.org)

Educational standards and tests (www.edstandards.org)

High school diploma requirements (www.homeschooldiploma.com)

College and university entrance requirements (www.homeeducator.com)

Available scholarships and grants (www.collegexpress.com)

Dual high school/college enrollment (www.ed.gov/offices/OVAE/CCLO/dualenroll.html)

Colleges that admit homeschoolers (www.learninfreedom.org)

Online college classes and degrees (www.classesusa.com)

Homeschool support and network groups (www.nhen.org)

Homeschool publications (www.covenanthome.com/pub_links.htm)

honest with yourself and with God. So you've made some mistakes. Okay! This is good! Don't you know success is built on mistakes?

Did you know that Thomas Edison had three hundred failed attempts before he produced a working filament for his electric lightbulb? Where would the high-tech, civilized, illuminated world be if he had been ashamed of his failures and given up? Did you know that before Lincoln was elected president he ran for virtually every other public office and lost? Do you think it was because he lacked leadership skills?

Don't be so quick to shoulder the blame and give up because you're ashamed that things haven't gone according to the script. It ain't over till it's over. Next week or next month could be so fabulous that it totally wipes away all the less-than-happy memories of your current ordeal.

Homeschoolers have an occupational hazard. We're all hyperactive, type A, obsessive-compulsive, over-achieving ultraperfectionists. Hey, that's why we homeschool in the first place. We can't settle for mediocre. We want more. And it had all better be just as flawless as Handel's "Hallelujah Chorus" sung by the angelic heavenly choir. So it just follows naturally, then, that when we discover our kids aren't the epitome of perfection, we're shocked! When we finally figure out we're not too perfect ourselves, we're even more shocked! Why? Because we've entertained visions of ourselves that bear no resemblance to reality.

It's like those photo-editing programs where you import the file of somebody's striking, professionally done, airbrushed portrait and have a heyday popping their eyebrows up into their hairline and dragging their earlobes down into their collar and their nostrils up into their eyelashes. Then you can really go to town by pulling a little here and giving them a nose like Jimmy Durante, and stretching a little there and giving them ears like Mr. Spock, then clicking and dragging over there and, bingo! They have eyes like Peter Lorre and a mouth like Boris Karloff.

Somehow we've created an equally distorted picture of ourselves and our abilities. In our fondest fantasy, we see ourselves as the virtuous woman from Proverbs 31.

I mean, who *is* this woman? Have you ever taken time to read her job description? She's Supermom the Magnificent, Defender of the Free Female World. She's Betty Crocker, Abigail Adams, Betsy Ross, and Florence Nightingale all rolled together, mind-melded with Jackie Kennedy and poured into a Barbie body. Everything in her life is under complete and serene control, her spotless house is on the cover of *Better Homes and Gardens,* and she's managing her husband's campaign for president.

He's on the cover of *Time.*

In her abundant periods of discretionary time, she single-handedly stocks and runs every burger franchise in three counties. When she prunes her prize-winning roses, not a trickle of sweat mars her flawless brow. Every wall in her house groans under such a prodigious array of homemade crafts that the wallpaper has all but disappeared, yet the effortless stream of art to sell at swap meets still flows forth. She pumps iron every day without fail and six times on Saturday, and hasn't gained an ounce since she was Miss America for three years running. Every fall she sews full back-to-school wardrobes for her perfectly behaved children.

These over-the-top demands we make of ourselves keep us firing on all twelve cylinders till we burn out. This is why we push our kids so hard. This is why we push ourselves so hard. This is why it's good to take an afternoon off now and then and go for a walk in the park. Sometimes you just have to look up at the blue sky out there and remember there's a great big God who loves you! It's therapeutic to take a stroll out onto the lake too and remember that you still can't walk on water.

Remember, homeschooling isn't all about you and what you perceive as your deficiencies, pedagogical or otherwise. Homeschool is all about you recognizing and accepting all your deficiencies and then trusting God to help you in spite of yourself.

Know Your Ally

The good news is we're not on our own. God is with us to provide discernment to see our kids' needs. He shows us what direction to take with each of them—how to approach those who are less approachable and reach those who are less reachable; how to bring out the best that he's placed within each of them as we partner with him. And we must remember that homeschooling, like parenting, is only a temporary engagement. God will be there for our children down the road too, as they're released to face educational situations outside our homes.

Ken and Bonnie Laue have always been part of the public school community. After years as a school bus driver, Ken has become one of the main bus route supervisors for his school district. Bonnie has taught special education for eighteen years in elementary schools and nine years in middle schools. When their daughters, Melissa and Michelle, were born, Bonnie took a five-year hiatus to stay home with them till they reached school age. Then, working in the same elementary schools they attended, she handpicked most of their teachers. These two factors played a crucial part in the success of her girls' early educational experiences.

Their older daughter pursued an exclusively public education.

"Melissa was quite happy to remain in the public schools," Bonnie says. "She worked hard, excelled academically, and was a witness for Jesus. She had no desire to be homeschooled, and I'm not sure how it would have played out for her in that setting."

Ken agrees: "As conservative Christian parents, we fought a number of battles and stayed involved in the process of her education at all times. We were gratified to see Melissa graduate high school with honors and scholarships, but even more to see her faith be a light in the darkness to her peers."

Though some of their friends were homeschooled, the Laues felt it wasn't for them. They felt that removing kids from the traditional school setting reduced their potential to witness to nonbelievers and to be the salt and light Jesus intended Christians to be.

But during Michelle's grade school career, her parents were obliged to take another look at homeschooling when they encountered outcome-based education.

"Friends had recommended this really great sixth-grade class," Bonnie says. "But apparently the whole plan for that class had changed over the summer. As the first quarter progressed and we saw Michelle's assignments and how they were graded, we became increasingly unhappy with the trend in that school.

"No textbooks were allowed, 'grades' were given on a rubric scale according to each student's personal best, the basics were not covered, and many times there was no right or wrong in the answers! She just wasn't making much progress."

Both parents were working then and had extensive ministry commitments at church. Although time seemed unavailable to homeschool, after much prayer they decided to try it. Bonnie got books for Michelle at the middle school where she worked, prepared her lessons, and graded them on weekends. Working at the home of a family friend, Michelle progressed quickly. While

49

content with homeschool that year, she wanted to try public school again for seventh grade.

Bonnie realized many of the teachers she chose were obliged to spend increasing amounts of class time dealing with discipline problems, and she doubted much progress could be made. Michelle felt she was indeed being held back, but stuck the year out. At her request, her folks agreed she could homeschool for eighth grade, and this time their fourteen-year-old daughter worked at her own home, alone.

"She was very self-motivated or I wouldn't have been able to let her work alone," says Bonnie. "This method won't work for everyone. Each child has different needs and rates of progress. Thankfully, Michelle's experience was a good one. She went on to complete public high school in three years instead of four, and entered community college. It was a lot of work for me, but looking back, I know it was worth the effort."

Michelle's older sister, Melissa, graduated from public high school as an honors student and went on to complete a bachelor's degree in journalism on a scholarship at the University of Arizona. Ken says that while conservative parents may fear for their kids in the prevailing atmosphere of corrupting liberalism at institutions of higher learning, God was with his daughter, and Melissa's personal convictions and faith saw her through without wavering.

Ken and Bonnie still serve in a district where 20 percent of the schools were recently labeled as "underperforming" by state and federal governments. But they have no regrets where their daughters' education is concerned.

"Don't be afraid to make the necessary sacrifices or to change what you're doing if it isn't meeting the children."[2]

Know Your Kids

When your kids are at risk, you want the best. Money's no object. Constraints of time and space are irrelevant. We're talking about your children; nothing is too much to ask. When it comes to knowing your kids, you need look no further than the mirror for the best. You want a specialist? You're it. You've known this kid from the first wiggle in the womb. You two were in sync way before the first diaper.

Just like Ken and Bonnie, you're the first to know when the flashing lights go off, and you're the one who cares enough to invest the time and effort to see your children succeed. The experts can't begin to fathom the stake you've sunk here. They can't wait around like you have and struggle with a late-blooming reader long enough to see her rocket through the newspaper or the Bible when she finally gets it. They must test and rate the kids' apparent abilities.

But IQ tests designed to test logic won't reveal a thing about a child who's a sensitive, creative, right-brained artist. Time is short, and teachers gravitate toward the easy students who are the great spellers and effortless writers and frown on the ones who struggle writing a two-sentence thank-you note to Gramps. They may miss the fact that these kids can excel in math and science and may wind up engineering their next computer upgrade.

In their book *Give Your Child a Superior Mind,* German educators Siegfried and Therese Engelmann say they've found the following to be true about intelligence test results:

> These tests involve only knowledge that is independent of surroundings. Telephone operators may score high on those IQ questions that measure the ability to repeat a series

of numbers such as "2 5 6 3 4 8 0 1 5," but idiot savants (severely retarded children who have developed a strange set of rules about language) have fantastic rote memories and can repeat even longer number strings. As isolated knowledge, this doesn't show the intellectual capacity. A boy raised in the country may find it impossible to memorize sets of dates in historical references, but be able to demonstrate fantastic ability at finding his way through the woods to a cabin or assembling the parts of an engine for a tractor. In other words, experiential knowledge.[3]

In her book *Anyone Can Homeschool,* Terry Dorian, Ph.D., points out the unique vantage point of a parent who knows his child, in contrast to the perception of traditional teachers: "Learning styles—how a child processes information—become pivotal in the homeschool. But in the classroom, they are a nuisance that hinders uniformity and order."[4]

Parents also know their children's individual quirks and their soft spots that must be protected until a healthy self-confidence can grow. Too often these are the very areas that are held up for ridicule in an early classroom—if not by the other children, then by the teacher. Kids even suffer ridicule because they're smart, and that makes them different—a sad commentary on the prevailing level of public education. In his book *Growing Up Learning,* Walter B. Barbre, Ph.D., says:

> One of the sure signs of being an adult is knowing just what you are weak in. No one will ever catch us doing something willingly, especially in front of others, that we know we don't do well. Our children are not so lucky. [Endlessly being confronted by their failures] can destroy their self-confidence and their willingness to learn.[5]

It takes a parent to see the diamond in a lump of coal. Practice visualizing those diamonds next time your little lumps traipse through the house, leaving clouds of coal dust in their wake. Michelangelo said he visualized the statue inside the slab of marble and that his job was to remove all the excess. Visualize and hone. That's what real teachers do. The caring, mentoring kind of teacher. The kind that's hard to find in the public education system these days. When you find them, cherish them as eternal friends; they deserve all your praise and adoration. Don't let them go unappreciated.

Every year our hometown hosts the fabulous Tucson Gem and Mineral Show. In 1988 an amateur rock collector at this show sold an egg-sized, violet-and-blue stone to a Texas gemologist for ten dollars. After months of rigorous appraisals, the gemologist announced that the rock was a 1905-carat star sapphire with an estimated uncut value of $2.28 million. It takes a guy who really knows his gems to pick them out of the rough.

A well-trained eye makes all the difference between the rock hound and the gemologist. The difference is in the ability and desire to see and develop potential. It's so much easier to label a child with a learning disability or emotional disorder than it is to be patient enough to recognize a different personality, a different style of learning, an out-of-the-ordinary intelligence, or a blooming creativity.

Who do you think gets the better educational results?

Sam B. Peavey, Ed.D., prepared a report for the Iowa State Board of Education in 1989 in which he reflected on the relatively young phenomenon of home-based education. He wrote: "It has been most interesting to me to see homeschool parents with high school diplomas doing as well or better than my certified teachers, as measured by their students' standardized test results. Those parents revealed some things to me about living, loving and learning, that I was never taught by my distinguished professors at Harvard and Columbia."[6]

Kids aren't cloned; each is unique, an individual with exclusive trademark capabilities and talents, gifting and intelligence. God will give you insight into how to use each of your kids' different quirks and strengths—and even their weaknesses—to help them absorb wisdom, inspiration, and knowledge.

Your children aren't produced on an assembly line and can't be run through a factory-style program where production doesn't stop for the individual. Custom work and quality results are only achieved by caring professionals; not by the mass-production assembly line putting out a standardized product for the chain franchise. Don't let the "powers that be" test your kids and stamp their foreheads with "slow" or "learning disabled" as they whiz by on the conveyor belt, because somehow they didn't fit the normal parameters. Tests are highly overrated.

In fact, in his book *Dumbing Down Our Kids: Why American Children Feel Good About Themselves But Can't Read, Write, or Add,* Charles J. Sykes says "learning disabilities" became the perfect explanation to parents for why their children could not read. It was the "educationists' equivalent of saying, 'Don't blame me,'" he says. "It wasn't the way we teach. It wasn't our abandonment of phonics. It wasn't our low standards, or the time we spent on making children feel good about themselves. It wasn't because we have stopped teaching children to acquire basic academic skills and figure they will pick them up on their own."[7]

Mother Murphy's Law #2: Those who think they can do it better than you messed it up when they had the chance.

James Madison said, "I believe there are more instances of the abridgement of freedoms of the people by the gradual and silent encroachment of those in power than by violent and sudden usurpations."[8] Simply put: Nobody wrestled the right to teach our kids away from us. We just handed that right over to them of our own free will, as the system convinced us of our own inabilities. That we have the inabilities is undeniable. That they're a pivotal issue in educating our offspring isn't.

During World War II, Hitler employed a tactic he called "the Big Lie." He broadcast false news over the airwaves reporting victory after victory for the Third Reich. To the soldiers fighting in the trenches, it sounded as if the Nazis were marching across Europe absolutely decimating the Allies.

It was an intimidation tactic designed to take the fight out of the guys on the front lines.

Parents in twentieth-century America were fed the Big Lie by the system: "Hands off. Don't touch it or you'll break it. Only we know how to teach your kids." In the enlightened twenty-first century, even frequent flyers on the information highway still feel inadequate to function in their natural parental role as educators of their own children.

Believing the Big Lie hasn't improved the educational state of our country. On the contrary: The system has done so well that we now hold the academic ticket to a back-row seat behind every other industrialized nation in the world.

During his administration, President Reagan commissioned a study on the appalling state of education in America. The National Commission on Excellence in Education called its report *A Nation at Risk*. Published in 1983, it acknowledged the parents' place as their child's natural teacher and issued an impassioned plea for them to be involved in their children's education:

> Your right to a proper education for your children carries a double responsibility. *As surely as you are your child's first and most influential teacher,* your child's ideas about

education and its significance begin with you. You must be a living example of what you expect your children to honor and to emulate. Moreover, you bear a responsibility to participate actively in your child's education. You should encourage more diligent study and discourage satisfaction with mediocrity and the attitude that says "let it slide" (emphasis added).[9]

The report included a section called "The Tools at Hand." The first tool listed was "the natural abilities of the young that cry out to be developed; and the undiminished concern of parents for the well-being of their children."[10] In other words, educational methods and personnel will come and go, but parents will always care enough to see their children make it.

Even in a private school setting, teachers aren't afforded the time to know each kid well enough to be familiar with the level of their capabilities. The Morenos' decision to homeschool came after deliberation and prayer, and after the realization that even in private schools, mediocrity is often rewarded.

Caitlin Moreno's teacher at her Christian school in Arizona had assigned the children to do a report on the Grand Canyon. Seizing the opportunity for an educational outing that would make a great memory, her parents put together a family trip to the natural wonder in their own backyard. Caitlin excitedly recorded her vivid firsthand experiences in a journal and on several rolls of film as the trip progressed. Upon arriving back home, she brought it all together into a magnificent report of which she was terribly proud.

The rest of the class, taking a more convenient route, relied on printouts of images and text from the Internet. They all got *A*'s. Caitlin got a *C*.

"This couldn't have been produced by your daughter," her parents were told upon questioning the grade. After sitting Caitlin down and requiring handwriting samples from her in order to match them with the writing on the posters, the instructor awarded her a reluctant *A*.

Spurred by this experience, the Morenos looked at other options but wondered if their children would be agreeable to home education.

"Your mother and I have prayed and talked," explained their dad, "and we've come to the conclusion that we'd like to try homeschooling sometime soon."

"Can we start tomorrow?" the kids said.[11]

While educational institutions may not be on the same page—or even in the same book—God can put the same desires into our children's hearts when it's his perfect time. And parents are already positioned as their kids' natural teachers.

"If you can teach your child how to dress himself, you can teach him academic skills," say the Engelmanns. "Even if your child gives no sign of being exceptionally bright, he can learn to read and to perform simple arithmetic operations before entering the first grade. Furthermore, if you consistently work with your child, he will become very smart."[12]

Think about it. You've been the first and most important instructor your kids have had. You've been teaching them from the word *go:* Say "Dada," tie your shoes, pick up your toys; learn hot from cold and up from down; learn your ABCs, learn your colors, learn algebra, learn quantum physics. So what's so different? You just keep right on teaching till you run out of things you know. By the time that happened at our place, we had a couple of kids already in college. And here's the serendipity: They became our resident tutors for the younger ones.

Thank God for grace!

Mother Murphy's Law #3: By the time you've got a handle on homeschooling, your kids are teenagers and you're back to square one.

Now we approach one of the scariest features of the homeschool ride: an inky black hole. The teenager tunnel looks so long!

Trust us: It's far longer than it appears.

Mark Twain said that all teenagers at age thirteen should be put into cracker barrels with the lid nailed shut and fed through a knothole. At seventeen, Twain advised, plug the knothole.

The word *adolescent* means "growing to adulthood," but the teenager knows he's already arrived. As homeschoolers, we ponder the ancient parental question that's plagued generations of our forebears: Why teach them anything when they know it all?

Push comes to shove when the suddenly omniscient teenager comes toe-to-toe with the mentally deficient parent or teacher who sees where the screws are still loose and is poised with screwdriver in hand to finish the job in the meager time allotted. Here's a perfect case of the irresistible force meeting the immovable object. This makes the teen years a fabulous time during which to improve parents' prayer lives.

The music. The car. The clothes. The job. The money they have no clue how to budget.

The parents, their knees now superglued to the carpet, go through various stages of response: Hurt. Depression. Self-examination and self-deprecation. Child-examination and child-deprecation. Anger. Despair. Hope. Deluded anticipation. Hopelessness. Pretended indifference. Callous resignation.

One day just a short forty-seven years later, the cocoon bursts and there emerges a beautiful, mature butterfly—a human being! He gives you a bear hug and admits to you that you really do exist. He acknowledges your years of effort invested in raising and homeschooling him. He may go as far as to verbally recognize you as a gift from God.

You hug him back, thanking God for his almighty grace. You dry your eyes, blow your nose, and wring out your sleeve.

You turn to your spouse.

"Hey, babe! Wanna go again?"

Lifesavers

1. Are you fighting your own battles? Do you lead the charge yourself? Then go for it! Ride against the enemy with your lance ready and your banners flying and get ready to be utterly decimated! Why? Because you can't trust you. Get smart: Make Jesus your captain and let him lead you to real victory under his banner.

Now I know that the LORD saves His anointed;
He will answer him from His holy heaven
With the saving strength of His right hand.
Some trust in chariots, and some in horses;
But we will remember the name of the LORD our
   God.
They have bowed down and fallen;
But we have risen and stand upright.

Psalm 20:6–8

Oh, GOD the LORD, the strength of my salvation,
You have covered my head in the day of battle.

Psalm 140:7

2. Remember the reality of you. That is, remember that your own strength is nonexistent and your best shot is inadequate:

For I know that in me (that is, in my flesh) nothing good dwells; for to will is present with me, but how to perform what is good I do not find.

Romans 7:18

Remember too that if you give up you and put on Christ, nothing is impossible:

What then shall we say to these things? If God is for us, who can be against us? Yet in all these things, we are more than conquerors through Him who loved us.

Romans 8:31, 37

3. Trust not in yourself, but in God, that your godly commitment to see your kids make it—academically and in all areas of life—coupled with your commitment to cling to God's almighty hand will see you through:

Glory in His holy Name;
Let the hearts of those rejoice who seek the LORD!
Seek the LORD and His strength;
Seek His face evermore!
Remember His marvelous works which He has done,
His wonders, and the judgments of His mouth.

Psalm 105:3–5

4. Moreover, when we admit how much we lack, God's grace makes up for our glaring deficiencies. As Jesus told the Pharisees, those who think they're well don't go to the doctor. Those who know they're sick do. James puts it this way:

But He gives more grace. Therefore He says:
"God resists the proud,
But gives grace to the humble."

James 4:6

3

Genius Builders
Anonymous

The Ex-Spurts

expert (ex'- spurt) *n.* A has-been drip under pressure.

Yes, you want to homeschool your kids. You see the need for it. You feel the desire. But you're afraid. Afraid you won't be able to handle it. Afraid you don't know enough. Afraid you don't know where to start or how to proceed. Afraid of yourself. Afraid of the kids. But most of all, afraid that educating your children should be left to "the experts."

Let's examine some famous quotes from the experts:

Decca Records executive at the Beatles's first audition: "They'll never make it. Guitar bands are on the way out."

Assessment of Fred Astaire by a New York talent agency:
"Uncoordinated. Can't sing. Can dance a little."

Estimate given by the chairman of IBM in 1943:
"There's a world market for about five computers."

In the early eighties, Bill "Mr. Microsoft" Gates said:
"640K [of memory] ought to be enough for anybody."[1]

Did you know that Thomas Edison's teachers kicked him out of grade school as a backward student unable to grasp the simplest concepts? Did you know that an early employer of Walt Disney's fired him for the inability to come up with creative ideas?

The ex-spurts sit on the committee of "they." *They* know how it should be done. *They* say you can't do it right. *They* sit in judgment of people who attempt to teach children without a teaching degree because *they* are the only qualified ones. *They* have been experimenting on your kids in the public school system for years and still can't agree on the one correct and effective method for teaching children properly.

But whatever it is, they're certain that parents can't possibly use it, because parents aren't the experts.

Contrary to the facade that the experts present, public education is not an exact science. On the contrary, it's dictated by fads and superstitions, by what's cool this week and what's not. Driven by peer pressure—like we try to teach our kids not to be—the experts change their educational methods at the drop of a hat.

Let's take a case in point: Remember word recognition? Perhaps you were a victim of this brilliant concoction. Perhaps you still are. This trend began when the experts came up with the brilliant premise that children who had just learned how to discern *A* from *B* shouldn't sound words out at all, but should read whole words at a glance. Because after all, adults read whole sentences at a glance! No problem: Just give the kid a list of words to memorize.

The only winners in this game were the privileged few blessed with photographic memory or total recall. If the word wasn't on the golden word list, the child was encouraged to take a wild guess. Spelling was dealer's choice. After all, if you don't know the letter sounds, how do you know what letter to put into this baffling word that's swirling around in your confused brain?

Before phonics regained a position of grace, that one innocent-looking educational fad produced an entire generation of adults who still can't write or spell and who have no desire to read a book even if they were able. And who can blame them? Reading this way can hardly be called relaxing.

Outcome-based education is the next greatest thing in popular education circles. This trendy approach features no educational standards, no tests, no textbooks, no grades, no report cards, and no holds barred. It's like removing the goalposts from the football field. Whatever you do, don't tell the child his work lacks a few yards. You may damage his ego.

Life in the Parallel Universe

You must remember that we live in today's child-centered society in which kids are never wrong, egotism is encouraged as "self-image," and the ultimate virtue is to be nonjudgmental—especially of sin. Take a look at the movie marquees; a hefty percentage of screenplays feature kids, and box office successes are often those that depict kids saving the world—usually from the bungling of some clueless adults who have made a royal mess of things.

Now lest you think this philosophy is restricted to the movies, take a look at how it's affected the schoolroom scenario: Kids no longer wait with folded hands upon their pristine desks for the teacher to enter so they can all rise as one body and chirp, "Good morning, Miss Smith." Tell a beleaguered instructor nowadays that this should occur, and you'll make her day. She'll have an uncontrollable fit of laughter. In fact, tell it to the kids in her classroom and watch them have the same fit.

Respect is no longer demanded of children in our society. In fact, it's demeaning to refer to them as *children*. They're supposed to be short adults, with all the rights and privileges afforded to taller adults. Kids today are treated as the teachers' peers—because they're treated as the peers of all adults—and their education has taken a backseat to making sure the child feels fairly treated. Therefore, children have little if any respect for their teachers, and far less discipline.

Now look at it from the teacher's point of view: If you give a kid a bad report card these days, he may pull a gun on you. If you encounter a child who might actually take the report card home and show it to her parents, you still lose, because you're making her accountable to the parents rather than to the state.

No, this isn't the school you went to. You can no longer tell your kids, "Well, when I was your age . . . ," because you've never been their age. In fact, you'll never be their age. They live in a different world where the rules under which you grew up no longer apply.

So if your child is currently in public school, ask yourself, Is my child learning anything? If not, it's time for a change. Remember: Don't care what the ex-spurts say. They still put their pants on one leg at a time. They've made more than their fair share of mistakes. Many were hardly noticeable. But others were big, ugly mistakes that have cost our kids dearly.

The Rest of the Story

In his September 1994 speech "Strong Families, Strong Schools," Secretary of Education Dick Riley said, "The family is the rock upon which solid education can and must be built."[2]

What? The family? Not the system?

These days, experts acknowledge that parents are vital to the educational process. The *Nation at Risk* report came out after a good twenty years of a philosophy that said only teachers knew what they were doing; parents didn't have a clue and they should not attempt this at home. When the report was released, it revealed the ultimate truth. The final outcome of this mind-set was a sad state of affairs:

If an unfriendly foreign power had attempted to impose on America the mediocre educational performance that exists today, we might well have viewed it as an act of war.[3] . . .

The ideal of academic excellence as the primary goal of schooling seems to be fading across the board in American education. On 19 academic tests American students were never first or second and, in comparison with other industrialized nations, were last seven times.[4] . . .

Some 23 million American adults are functionally illiterate by the simplest tests of everyday reading, writing and comprehension. About 13 percent of all 17-year-olds in the U.S. can be considered functionally illiterate . . . among minority youth [it] may run as high as 40 percent.

The average achievement of high school students on most standardized tests is now lower than 26 years ago when Sputnik was launched. Many 17-year-olds do not possess the 'higher order' intellectual skills we should expect of them. Nearly 40 percent cannot draw inferences from written material; only one-fifth can write a persuasive essay; only one-third can solve a Mathematics

65

problem requiring several steps. SAT scores demonstrate a virtually unbroken decline from 1963 to 1980.[5]

The report went on to say that "secondary school curricula have been homogenized, diluted, and diffused to the point that they no longer have a central purpose."[6]

The committee recommended that students seeking a diploma be required to "lay the foundations in the Five New Basics in high school."[7] Guess what the "new" basics were? English, math, science, social studies, and computer science. Of the five, perhaps the last was new.

But we live in a more enlightened educational world now, right? Hmm.

"Few of the ideas now being offered as 'reforms' and innovations are, in fact, new," says Sykes. "Most are retreads of notions fashionable in the 1920s, the 1940s and the 1950s, repackaged and renamed to obscure their discredited ancestries."[8]

But now, do you know what is new? One of the biggest modern educational trends is the involvement of parents in the classroom. Schools are now begging for parental participation. The eighth goal in the Goals 2000 Standards of Education is parental involvement. Mentoring and shadowing have become buzzwords among educators. Both of these carry the idea of matching students up with competent adult role models, says Charles S. Clark in his *CQ Researcher* article "Parents and Schools."[9] They're calling back in the pros.

Yes, parents are educators. You have a great background as an educator too. The truth is that home education is a thoroughly natural process in which you've been participating for quite some time now, whether the experts acknowledged it or not. As a parent, you've been teaching your kids since they took their first breath. With or without a degree, you taught them to speak (English), sang them lullabies (music appreciation), and taught them sandwich making and juice mixing (home economics).

In the story of *The Emperor's New Clothes,* a child blows the whistle on the world's first royal streaker. While adults denied that the monarch was indecently exposed, only the child had the guts to blow his cover, bringing instant enlightenment to the entire kingdom.

Such is the genius of those who dare tell the truth.

For years America suffered with a scantily clad educational system and the functionally illiterate fruits thereof. Finally homeschoolers got fed up. Yanking their kids out, they proved there was something better and exposed the nakedness of the committee of they.

Take Heart, Parent

Years of experience are already in your favor. Even institutions of higher learning now recognize you were more qualified than you thought you were.

A front-page headline in the February 11, 2000, *Wall Street Journal* announced: "Colleges Recruit Homeschooled Kids." The article introduced Jason Scoggins, who at seventeen was sought out for a full scholarship by Ogelthorpe University after having achieved 1570 out of 1600 possible points on his SAT with a perfect 800 in math. His twin brother, Jeremy, scored 1480. The *Journal* determined that these high scores for homeschoolers are no fluke and are becoming more and more commonplace. Ogelthorpe accepts top applicants for five scholarships valued at $100,000 apiece. Of the ninety-four prospects for the prizes in the January 2000 contest, eight were homeschoolers, each with SATs above 1300.

The article continues:

The SAT and the ACT have begun asking exam takers whether they were homeschooled. Homeschoolers have bettered the national averages on the ACT for the past three years running, scoring an average 22.7 last year compared with 21 for their more traditional peers, on a scale of one to 36. On the SAT homeschoolers scored an average 67 points above the national average. On the 10 SAT2 achievement tests most frequently taken by homeschoolers, they surpassed the national average on nine, including writing, physics and French. With average family incomes of $40,000 to $50,000, lower than the $50,000–$60,000 median rung, homeschoolers also defied the demographic correlation between high incomes and high SAT scores.[10]

Well, okay, but what about socialization? Won't these children become the isolated pod people that time forgot—shut away for so long that they're unable to relate to their peers?

On the contrary: Homeschoolers have conquered the halls of higher education and proven themselves the most mature natural leaders in every setting. Why? Because they've been trained in their homes to be real, live, thinking, mature adults.

The same *Wall Street Journal* article tells of Maggie Bryson, the first homeschooler to win Ogelthorpe's full scholarship in 1999 at the age of fifteen. (Jason was the 2000 winner.) "With a 1430 SAT score, including 800 on the verbal, she applied to eight colleges and was accepted at seven, including Ogelthorpe. Now a freshman, Ms. Bryson has an A-minus average and is teaching herself Arabic and ancient Egyptian hieroglyphics in her spare time."[11]

The level of self-confidence achieved through being comfortable in one's adulthood was what the *Journal* described as Bryson "still adapting to classroom etiquette." "We homeschoolers tend to be very vocal and talk to the professor directly," the *Journal* quotes her as saying, noting her afterthought, "It might bother the other students a little bit."[12]

Jason offers his own theory on education: Public schools will never excel because they "lack intellectual capital." To soften the blow, he allows that they have to compensate for many social problems, but he then raises a question as to whether they should be found in the position to do so: "They have different educational programs that take away from the three R's, and the parents don't care enough," he affirms. "I know it's said that schools should be centers of socialization. But that's not their role. Their role is to impart knowledge."[13]

Historically Speaking

You may recognize a name here and there in the following list of homeschooled children: Thomas Edison, Albert Einstein, Benjamin Franklin, Patrick Henry, C. S. Lewis, Wolfgang Amadeus Mozart, Blaise Pascal, Leonardo DaVinci, Abraham Lincoln, Franklin D. Roosevelt, Teddy Roosevelt, Clara Barton, Florence Nightingale, Woodrow Wilson, Dwight L. Moody, Winston Churchill, Pearl S. Buck, George Washington Carver, Hans Christian Andersen, Agatha Christie, William Penn, Samuel Clemens (Mark Twain), Laura Ingalls Wilder, George and Martha Washington, Pierre and Marie Curie, Gen. Douglas MacArthur, Alexander Graham Bell, Daniel Webster, Orville and Wilbur Wright, and Sally Ride.[14]

The truth is that public education didn't exist until the nineteenth century. At the dawn of the United States, home education was the norm. In the colonies, one-room schoolhouses eventually grew out of parental education. According to James C. Carper, Ph.D., "Home instruction dominated the educational configuration of colonial

America and continued to a lesser extent throughout the nineteenth century."[15]

In other words, there were no public schools. The founding fathers weren't produced by public education. Yet they put together a working democratic government still unrivaled anywhere on earth.

Abe Lincoln never attended public schools, but he had the common sense and moral convictions to abolish slavery as a godless practice, held a nation together through the Civil War, and at the end acknowledged, "All I am I owe to my angel mother."

These leaders weren't products of the employee factories we have today, whose success is measured in job placement. They didn't come to the New World salivating over a minimum wage job and a position behind a fast-food counter. They were tutored as independent thinkers who knew how to fight for God and for freedom. Two centuries later the free nation they founded is still the envy of the world.

Maria Montessori (1870–1952) was the first woman medical doctor in Italy and pioneer of a preschool educational method. She said a child learns best by doing, that a child has a natural desire to know, and that the teacher must develop a child's intelligence and imagination into curiosity, which is a prerequisite for creative learning. Historically, that teacher was a parent.

John Wesley Taylor, Ph.D., a professor of education, says:

> The home is mankind's first and most basic school. Home-centered education is as old as civilization itself, commencing long before state schools were organized or even conceived. Throughout much of American history, the primary center of instruction was the family. Parents were frequently the sole instructors for their offspring. The home is an ideal environment for fostering creativ-

ity, inquiry and practical learning . . . the child is given a chance to explore and discover. He participates in active learning—the doing. He can experience learning—not just read or hear about it. He learns how to learn.[16]

Historian Steven Mintz and anthropologist Susan Kellogg say in *Domestic Revolutions: A Social History of American Family Life* that what a child learns at home forms the basis of his or her entire future interactions in society:

> Three centuries ago the American family was the fundamental economic, educational, political, social and religious unit of society. The household was not only the focus of production, it was also the institution primarily responsible for the education of children, the transfer of craft skills, and the care of the elderly and infirm.[17]

Historical evidence, coupled with the academic deficiency achieved since early practices were abandoned, provides an astounding revelation: The experts don't know as much as they make out. And as for the outcome of your child, you're the one who cares. You're the one who will cheer them on. You're the one who will be there at the finish line.

You're the real expert.

All in the Original Greek Means "All"

You know why you're more expert than the experts? Not only are you your child's first and most natural and effective teacher; not only do you get unique input opportunities in your child's first and most impressionable years of life before age six; not only are you most sensitive to your children's different personalities and points of receptivity. On top of all that, you have the inside track to the giver of all wisdom and knowledge (James 1:5). You're plugged into the power source that the experts have yet to find. You're on the winning team, and nothing can separate you from the love of God, which is in Christ Jesus, our Lord (Rom. 8:39).

Nothing! Not even homeschooling!

When the cat has hacked up a hairball on the carpet, and the baby is teething, drooling, and wiping her nose on the couch cushions, and the kids haven't gotten through their first subject by six o'clock on the night your mother-in-law's coming over for dinner, God will be there for you. Ask me how I know. Nothing can separate you from the love of God. And *that* is why you can do it.

John Gray became famous for his book called *Men Are from Mars, Women Are from Venus.* Or in other words, What Planet Are *You* From? I highly recommend it, by the way. It's a best-seller because it's so true! We just don't speak the same language. Marital bliss would be a piece of wedding cake if we never opened our mouths. Obviously, this isn't a viable solution, but it would sure cut down on marriage counseling bills!

But miscommunication can also happen when *God* talks to us. If we don't get what he's saying, we stand to miss out on a whole heap of blessings! For instance, that *all things* clause back in Romans 8:32. Right next to where God's just said he's for you and so who can be against you, and that you're more than a conqueror through him who loved you—God promised you *all things.* Remember?

Pull out that lexicon again. What does *all things* mean in the original Greek text?

I'm of the opinion that it means *all* things. Even things like the ability to homeschool our kids. Why do you let the devil bully you into thinking you can't? The way to handle the bully is to call in your big brother Jesus to take him on.

Practical atheists are folks who profess to know God but go about living as though he didn't exist. People who don't pray are practical atheists. These folks must have a death wish; they choose to go it alone.

Okay, I know. Rambo wipes out whole armies with his one-man portable arsenal. That's why he lives in Hollywood. In the real world, you'd be hitting the dirt. Your real secret weapon is down there in the foxhole: the EKA (elephant knees anointing). The more time you spend down there wrinkling those babies in prayer, the more backup you get from heaven. Now that's what I call survival of the fittest!

Yes, Christians do have the edge. But we only rock because God rules. He rules in our hearts and in our homes. He rules every time we hit our knees before him and ask him to help us and give us his wisdom from above for our homeschool beneath. He rules when we teach our kids to ask him for help in their schoolwork.

Never start a day of schoolwork without praying alone and with your kids. Encourage them to read their own Bibles and pray every morning, seeking their own power from God. If they're still too young to read the Bible, set aside time to read to them and lead them in prayer. Soon they'll be able to fly solo, and by then they'll know where to turn when they need help and power for living.

God says in James 1:5 that he's just waiting for you to say the word so he can break out with the wisdom you need for teaching, and Proverbs 9:10 shows us where that wisdom starts: "The fear of the LORD is the beginning of wisdom, and the knowledge of the Holy One is understanding."

Remember: However little you feel you know, you still know more than your kids.

Do you expect to know everything up front? Can you pour the Pacific Ocean into your sand castle on the beach? Do your headlights shine all the way to New York when you leave San Francisco Bay? Enlightenment comes a little piece of the road at a time. Don't worry: You'll learn right along with those guys. I finally wound up knowing something after going through high school eight times with ours.

Share what you know with your kids till you run dry, then read up, pray up, and give out some more. Gather all your vessels and watch God fill them with Holy Spirit oil as you keep pouring it all out (2 Kings 4:3–4).

Enabling the Drive

In spite of everything we've discussed, we must have a compassionate outlook on the state of the classroom in the twenty-first century. Teachers have so little backup that it's a major accomplishment just to keep kids within four walls, let alone teach them. Let's face it: If an educator these days is faced with a kid who has an ego the size of Texas and no desire to be enlightened, he or she has a tough row to hoe. After everything else teachers have to put up with, extending themselves for the child's benefit is more than they can achieve. It's hard to know the right buttons to push to motivate such a child.

Tina Lewis is a Tucson homeschooler who discovered that when it comes to button pushing, a parent has the inside track. "Every conference I had with Eric's kindergarten teacher," she explains, "she'd tell me he couldn't recognize his lowercase letters and didn't know the names of them. I told her that I knew he did, because I'd taught them to him myself. I knew he was just playing games with her."

"Look," Tina told the teacher, "you can take away his recess period or whatever is needed to motivate him, because he does know these letters, and he just doesn't feel like telling you."

The situation continued. At every conference until the last one of the year, the teacher asserted that this was a hole in Eric's understanding that he just couldn't get through.

"It bothered me enough that I thought maybe he'd somehow truly forgotten them," Tina says. "So I came home from that last conference and gave him a test myself. We played it like a bingo game, and I promised him a prize if he'd tell me his lowercase letters."

"I don't know, I don't know!" said Eric, using what was now his automatic reply.

"If you don't tell me your lowercase letters and sounds right now," said his mother, "you're going to take a nap with your two baby brothers."

He whipped those letters out within two seconds.[18]

Tina had the mom's edge. She knew her son; she knew the proper leverage to use. So what will happen when you're not around, parent? Do you just send them off and trust that they'll be motivated to learn when nobody's issuing the challenge? If a kid's not in learning mode and you don't know how to get him there, you lose.

When it comes to button pushing, a parent knows best.

There are precious jewels here and there—teachers we can all remember who have cared and gone the extra fifty miles for us, after hours and on their own time, and who have thereby made a difference in our scholastic history. But the caring individuals who have actually put the time into cultivating the tougher sod are rare indeed.

Most teachers face a classroom of forty-plus kids at the shallow end. They'll never be able to direct specialized attention to any one of them. No wonder more and more "special needs" classes pop up. Smaller classes are the only settings in which this sort of focused, individualized attention is possible. For the most part, today's kids are just swept along till they fall through the cracks and are left behind, or until they're added to the growing numbers of the "disabled." Herein lies one of the greatest benefits of the small homeschool class.

Now, I daresay my kids are just like yours. None of them was so specially gifted that they woke up salivating to tear into quantum physics each morning at the age of three. Every one of them had off days when they stared at the Jell-O dripping down the wall and finished maybe one subject by dinnertime. Sometimes they had whole off weeks, making me certain the invasion of the body snatchers had replaced my diligent protégés with inferior occupants.

To a parent, even in these extreme circumstances, the solution to the "I don't wanna learn" problem is simple: Make the kid crazy about learning. How? By making him confident of his ability to learn. By challenging him and getting him totally caught up in the thrill of discovery. By rewarding her moments of revelation. By telling her how perceptive she is and how special her knowledge will be to the world. That's right: Just talk 'em up, Mom.

Then go to the back room, shut the door, collapse on the bed in tears, and ask your husband why their brains just aren't in gear and why they're driving you crazy today, because you just know they can do this stuff!

Okay. Enough of that. Get up right now and go look in the mirror. What's staring back at you is the rock upon which solid education can and must be built. Yeah, you! But not just you. The real Rock: Christ in you, the hope of glory (Col. 1:27).

Pity parties are an easy option when you're just looking at you. You can think of yourself as just another stay-at-home mom or rise up and realize who you really are in Jesus. You can realize you've achieved a stellar position as a top-notch executive who's mastered multitasking much better than all those guys in the Armani suits who

A Day in the Life

Disclaimer: This is the rarely experienced perfect-day scenario . . . but we keep trying!

6:30–7:30 Wake up, personal devotions, dress, and make bed.

7:30–8:15 Summon the troops. Make lessons while chores are done.

8:15–8:45 Announce breakfast. Phone calls and laundry. Breakfast cutoff.

8:45–8:55 Fifteen-minute warning. Dishes and cleanup. Room checks.

8:55–9:00 Five-minute warning. Call for lesson-time prayer.

9:00–9:45 First period (Mom teaches younger grades. Phone off hook.)

9:45–10:00 First break (Mom corrects lessons and checks messages.)

10:00–10:45 Second period (Mom teaches. No phone.)

10:45–11:00 Second break (Mom corrects and checks.)

11:00–12:00 Third period (Mom teaches. No phone.)

12:00–1:00 Lunch break (Mom corrects and rewards all finished by lunch. Phone back on.)

1:00–1:45 Fourth period (Mom does daily work list, and older siblings tutor younger.)

1:45–2:00 Fourth break (All encouraged to finish no later than this for prize.)

2:00–3:00 Fifth period (Those left after this work till finished. No more breaks.)

3:00–5:00 Projects, outings, calls, paperwork, shopping, etc.

5:00–6:00 Dinner preparation and latter-end cleanups.

6:00–9:00 Dinner and evening family or church activities.

9:00–9:30 Family devotions. Kids' bedtime.

9:30–10:30 Mom and Dad hour. Bedtime.

offer expensive workshops on the subject. How would they do simultaneously teaching the kids, cleaning the house, answering the phone, balancing the checkbook, and stirring the spaghetti sauce?

Remember to focus on God and see yourself as who you are in him. Not as the person the world perceives you to be. Yes, I know: We know who we really are. I know me. I know I'm nothing. But that's a good place to be, because then I can get back down there on my knees and beg God for grace and wisdom from above.

The experts make a fatal mistake: They trust in human wisdom. When man stumbles upon one of the laws of the universe that God put into place from the foundation of the world, he gets so excited he forgets himself. He forgets who he is and who God is. Man begins to get things a little backward and thinks he's so smart and God's so out of the picture. He forgets who is omnipotent and who is puny. He kicks God out of the public schools and sandblasts God's commandments off the walls of the courts. He confuses freedom of religion with freedom *from* religion. He erects a monument to the wisdom of man.

My favorite picture of the monument to human wisdom follows here, in the form of a poem by Percy Bysshe Shelley:

Ozymandius

I met a traveler from an antique land,
Who said—Two vast and trunkless legs of stone
Stand in the desert. Near them, on the sand,
Half sunk a shattered visage lies, whose frown
And wrinkled lip, and sneer of cold command
Tell that its sculptor well those passions read
Which yet survive, stamped on these lifeless things.
The hand that mocked them, the heart that fed;
And on the pedestal these words appear:
"My name is Ozymandius, king of kings.

Look on my works, ye mighty, and despair!"
Nothing beside remains. Round the decay
Of that colossal wreck, boundless and bare
The lone and level sands stretch far away.

"The truth will set you free," said the one and only King of kings, Jesus Christ (John 8:32 NIV). And the real truth is, nobody ranks higher than you as the expert on your own children. The real truth is, you have the goods—the wisdom and power of God, not the deficient methodology of man. The real truth is, you are duty and honor bound to answer the William Tell calling given you by God in Psalm 127:4: "Like arrows in the hand of a warrior, so are the children of one's youth."

Wow. Notice it doesn't say "like students in the hands of a pedagogue." God chose *you*. He chose you out of all the parents in the world and put you together with your kids, whom he chose out of all the children in the world, to create a perfect fit. Those little arrows are your unique area of expertise. They're placed in your quiver at birth. You get the first shot.

You aim 'em. You shoot 'em. You watch God guide 'em to hit the bull's eye.

Genius Builders

Homeschooling is an extension of parenting, not a function of credentials. *Expertise* by definition implies that an area of specific knowledge has been mastered by a person who has done long hours of in-depth study accompanied by field trials and who is now finally qualified to wear that title and deserve it. When it comes to your personal offspring, who is more expert at knowing your children than their parent? Who has lived with them since birth, watched them develop, met their needs, and

79

learned what makes them tick? Who has a vested interest in what information goes into their brains and what ultimately comes out? Who will care if they're protected and cared for and if they live godly lives?

When push comes to shove over the well-being of these kids, paid hirelings will hit the road, leaving the natural shepherd who has been gifted by God with the necessary loving concern (John 10:12) and is willing to make early and abundant deposits into the children's lives.

Does deliberate early input really make a difference? Won't those kids take off and learn just as quickly once they hit school, regardless of the up-front input and without all that extra work? The hard evidence says no. Siegfried and Therese Engelmann cite the example of "genius builder" Karl Witte, an Austrian clergyman who made this claim to a circle of his pedagogical friends: "If God grants me a son, and if he, in your own opinion, is not to be called stupid—I have long ago decided to educate him to be a superior man, without knowing in advance what his aptitudes may be."[19]

Bold words, to say the least. But Witte stood by them when he had a son.

At the outset, his wife thought her husband's efforts were a waste of time and that the boy was, in fact, dull. But what had been a slow infant and a fairly normal four-year-old became an exceptional six-year-old, then an astonishing nine-year-old.

The following unabashed praise came in a letter sent by one of Witte's doubting friends when young Karl was a boy of ten: "I see him now in manly maturity, with childlike innocence and goodness in rare union—a charming picture of ennobled humanity! O lead me into a room filled with such men, and I shall deem myself to be removed from earth and in the company of higher spirits!"

The verdict was in: The boy Karl had become a superior man indeed. He entered Leipzig at nine, received a Ph.D. at fourteen, and earned a Doctor of Laws at sixteen—at which point he was immediately appointed to the teaching staff of the University of Berlin. By twenty-three he was a full professor at the University of Breslau, where he remained for the rest of his life, building a reputation as teacher, writer, and scholar.[20] Karl's dad had built a genius.

Such genius builders exist today and are known as homeschoolers.

Sam Peavey said in his recommendations to the Iowa State School Board:

> The intimacy and affection found in healthy homes provide the ideal basis, environment and catalyst for learning. Do not underestimate what you bring to your child as a teacher. You have been with him since the day he was born. You know what he struggles with and what he's good at. You know what motivates him and what discourages him. Parents are in unique positions to discover the genius in each child.[21]

In other words, it's only natural: Education in all aspects of life must begin in the home and is most effective when administered to young children by loving parents who care the most about them.

Montessori said that children effortlessly soak in everything in their culture and environment and should therefore have respectful, stimulating, nurturing, and meaningful direction and guidance during the "absorbent mind stage."[22] One thing the experts have gotten right is that their "sponge state" ends at age five—about the age they hit traditional schools.

As parents and children explore the wonders of God's fantastic world together, all the academic disciplines come into play: science, language, social skills, creativity, problem solving, thought processes, and decision making. The list is endless. Bet you didn't know you were such a great teacher with such fabulous potential.

Let the vacuum cleaner and dust cloth collect cobwebs in the closet for a while. Let the dishes actually reach the sink edge and let the laundry reach the top of the basket. The house you have with you always, and whenever you like you can do good unto it. The kids will be past the sponge state before you know it, and as we all know, parents instantly become mentally deficient on a child's thirteenth birthday. Sometimes sooner.

Make geniuses while the sun shines.

Lifesavers

1. If the ex-spurts have gotten you down, the kids have had "one of those days," the house is a wreck, and you've had a bad hair day—just call a recess, shut yourself into the bathroom, wash your face, brush your hair, breathe in and out, and thank God that somehow you're still alive (after a fashion). Then latch onto this truth and remember who you really are:

But you are a chosen generation, a royal priesthood, a holy nation, His own special people, that you may proclaim the praises of Him who has called you out of darkness into His marvelous light.

1 Peter 2:9

And never forget why it is that you can do it:

I can do all things through Christ who strengthens me.

Philippians 4:13

2. Next time you're worried about how much you don't know and how much the ex-spurts really seem to have it together and you don't, remember:

For you see your calling, brethren, that not many wise according to the flesh, not many mighty, not many noble, are called. But God has chosen the foolish things of the world to put to shame the wise, and God has chosen the weak things of the world to put to shame the things which are mighty; and the base things of the world and the things which are despised God has chosen, and the things which are not, to bring to nothing the things that are, that no flesh should glory in His presence. But of Him you are in Christ Jesus, who became for us wisdom from God—and righteousness and sanctification and redemption—that, as it is written, "He who glories, let him glory in the LORD."

1 Corinthians 1:26–31

3. Paul the apostle had the privilege of blowing the whistle on the educational emperor's new clothes of his own time. Having learned at the feet of the great teacher Gamaliel, he was thoroughly qualified to know scriptural wisdom when he heard it. And also when he didn't. Paul said:

Where is the wise? Where is the scribe? Where is the disputer of this age? Has not God made foolish the wisdom of this world? Because the foolishness of God is wiser than men, and the weakness of God is stronger than men.

1 Corinthians 1:20, 25

4. In order to succeed at our genius-building endeavor, we must attack the job head-on and remember we're building excellence as God gives us grace to do so. The outcome is a testimony to the world:

And whatever you do, do it heartily, as to the Lord and not to men.

Colossians 3:23

Let your light so shine before men, that they may see your good works and glorify your Father in heaven.

Matthew 5:16

You're So Lucky You're Homeschooled!

The Rolls Royce of Education

Ogelthorpe University's admissions director, Barbara Henry, admits that she used to dismiss homeschoolers as crackpots.[1] Now the tables are turned, and more institutions are regarding the product of these homespun efforts with new eyes.

And why not? After all, these students have had the benefit of years of personal tutoring, the most effective type of one-on-one learning possible. The kind of personal attention usually available only to the privileged upper crust and only at an exorbitant price.

By the early 1980s the public was ready for a change. Traditional classroom delivery methods had failed. Few remaining educators viewed teaching as a calling rather than a paycheck. Even fewer afforded their pupils any real one-on-one time, and that usually had to occur during unpaid overtime hours as a labor of love. In 1983 the government report *A Nation at Risk* finally gave the homeschool community a shot at popularization and supplied the momentum it needed.

Schooling one's own children at home offered the downsized classroom and the concerned tutor that had become painfully absent in the public school setting. Disappointed by failing academic results, parents stepped up to the plate.

In her book *Anyone Can Homeschool,* Terry Dorian points out the advantages of one-on-one learning:

> Students learning at home under the tutelage of a parent can progress at their own pace, regardless of ability. In effect, each student has an Individual Educational Plan (IEP), which is implemented in the classroom only for special needs students because of time and expense.[2]

Educators Siegfried and Therese Engelmann say private tutoring produces noticeable IQ gains, not uncommonly as high as fifteen to twenty-five points after only a year of such tutoring, regardless of the method used.[3]

All this evidence is fine and good, but your manicurist, your neighbor, your auto mechanic, and your mother-in-law all frown upon homeschooling and are sure it will do more academic harm than good to your offspring. They'll put an arm around your shoulders with a condescending cluck of the tongue and assure you that you can't do it.

So, why do you listen to these people?

When Igor Sikorsky was a lad of twelve, his parents told him that competent scientific authorities had proven mechanical flight impossible. Obviously Sikorsky chose to ignore this valuable information, as he invented and built the first helicopter. In his American helicopter plant, he posted a sign, which read, "According to recognized aero-technical tests, due to the shape and weight of his body in relation to total wing area, the bumblebee cannot fly. But the bumblebee doesn't know this. So he flies anyway."[4]

Most often we don't rise to the challenge because we're afraid of ruffling a few feathers in the status quo. Believe me: Those birds haven't fluffed those tail feathers in way too long. They could use a good ruffling. Be proud to be the catalyst that blows them off the branch. Be proud to be a force for positive change. You can only say "I made it through the rain" if you have the courage to slap on a raincoat and pick up an umbrella. Trust me: You'll need that protection if you're stepping out and making a difference. It won't happen if you huddle under the awning with the fainthearted. True leaders check out what the masses are doing and then step out and do the opposite.

Tutoring is the Rolls Royce of education, producing a custom-built model superior to the assembly-line product because it's built with TLC. Friends of ours who are lifetime career public education experts personally chose homeschooling for their own kids. That says something about educators in the know and exactly what they know about public education.

I say chuck that Chevy and get yourself a Rolls.

Fish and Chips at Eighty-eight Miles per Hour

Homeschooling helps kids excel academically for the simple reason that they gain confidence that they can absorb knowledge on their own. Rather than being spoon-fed prechewed data by a teacher, they quickly find they can learn anything worthwhile using the nontraditional methods that work best for them. In short, they've become their own highly effective teachers.

So says my brother, Steve Badaracco, who after declining a college education has worked for years as a self-taught senior computer programmer for major financial institutions.

He and his wife, Janet, have homeschooled their girls for seventeen years. As this book is released, Sara graduates college just as Laura finishes high school and Becca completes eighth grade.

Here they share with us one of their success stories that grew from the academic flexibility of their homeschool setting:

In fifth grade, Sara was drowning in lists of spelling words when we found a book at our favorite curriculum fair, the garage sale. She learned from this obscure college text to analyze patterns and to think how a new word was likely to be spelled instead of memorizing it. That summer we strolled into the mall one Saturday to find the food court packed—standing room only. The Encyclopedia Britannica organization was holding a regional spelling bee.

Sara walked up to where the action was, and they registered her on the spot. For the next hour and a half, scores of local kids butchered our already mangled language. When the dust cleared, Sara and the other remaining girl continued spelling words I'm sure don't exist outside the fevered brains of spelling-bee scriptwriters. In the end, Sara took second place and her new friend took first. Paparazzi crowded around and shoved microphones in their faces to ask their ages.

"What school do you attend?" asked the Britannica chap.

"Homeschool," Sara said.

"The Home School? Haven't heard of that one," he said. "Is it here in Saratoga Springs?"

"Of course," she replied. "It's in my *home!*"

"Our daughter is homeschooled too," said the other girl's parents. "Through last year."

"I didn't know kids could be homeschooled nowadays," said the Britannica rep, "but I can't argue with success. There must be something to it!"

I heard about a fellow in the UK who distills vegetable oil, dumps it into his gas tank, and cruises town in his Mercedes smelling like a fish-and-chips restaurant. The engine's confused enough that it thinks nothing of it, and the man never buys a pint of diesel, thank you very much.[5]

So how come the rest of us don't buy our gas at the grocery store? Because as "Doc" Brown told Marty McFly in *Back to the Future III*, "You're just not thinking fourth-dimensionally!" If the good ol' way just has to be best, we won't consider alternative fuels. After all, Doc's DeLorean ran on garbage. He didn't understand why Marty wouldn't get behind the wheel and careen off a cliff into midair at eighty-eight mph because Doc thought fourth-dimensionally. He knew Marty would land on a bridge constructed a hundred years in the future. No sweat.

But as Marty put it, "Yeah, I have a real problem with that."

Don't we all? Flying off cliffs is a standard entry on the resumé of those aspiring to great conquests. The West. Mount Everest. Space. And greatest of all, the Next Generation. Are these conquests possible? Of course not! Not by conventional means. Remember the Gordian Knot.

The conventional "wisdom" must be discarded on the faith that higher and more reliable wisdom will carry us across the chasm. When we step outside the realm of the familiar, the boundaries disappear.

Homeschool parents know the secret effectiveness of alternative fuel: The grace of God will guide unique individuals through individually tailored plans that help each learn best, and thereby broaden their horizons. When we careen off that cliff into the unknown, we find our kids' Creator has a bridge in place to take them safely across the chasm to the future he's prepared for them. Isaiah said, "All thy children shall be taught of the LORD; and great shall be the peace of thy children" (Isa. 54:13 KJV). I'll power my homeschool with that fuel any day.

Janet and I set out over the cliff in 1986. Like all homeschool parents, we judged ourselves least likely to succeed. Janet never finished college, and I've never had a day of it. We worried that our kids would become social misfits and we'd become mean teachers. We hired brass bands to get them out of bed and implemented every conceivable wall chart for motivation.

But do traditional school families get to pledge allegiance to a twelve-inch American flag together every morning? Do they take off for a four-week RV tour of America's national parks in early September as part of their curriculum? These are the defining marks of the new species—*homeschooler*. The cons designed to intimidate America away from the alternative education fuel pump are mere shadow bogeys to this resilient bunch, and we're here to stay.[6]

Watch for Detours

God knows that all families are dysfunctional. We prefer the term *unique*. And within each family, each individual is unique. It stands to reason, then, that if we stuff them into a one-size-fits-all educational program, many round pegs will have trouble fitting with the squares. Part of a parent's job is to pull those pegs out when they see the smooth edges are in danger of damage and defacement.

This gives a parent yet another advantage in homeschooling: giving each unique child the emotional stability he or she needs, and thus the strength for success in their social interactions as adults.

Oregonian columnist Sheila Hagar writes of an impromptu visit to her daughter's school that solidified her decision to homeschool:

At Home in School

Living in the schoolhouse and schooling in the home

When school's out, home should be homey. The place can't be done in "Early American one-room schoolhouse," but the kids can't stay in "endless vacation fried-brain-at-home mode" either.

Here are some ways to draw the fine line:

Lesson stations: Dining room tables suit multiple young scholars because the upper grades' reading lessons provide background music for the toddlers' flash-card sessions. We never kept hard-and-fast stations, though. Each kid's set of schoolbooks lived in a box, and we rotated them frequently to avoid boredom. Bedroom desks served for independent students, and kitchen counters near Mom were for scholars who fought to focus.

Bulletin boards / displays: Corkboards or the fridge may showcase exceptional work. Occasional hallway art galleries are fun too. But for year-round use, posters are tops. In bedrooms and hallways we displayed anything from manners, days of the week, and the order of the planets to pictorials of geometric shapes and the fallacies of evolution. You may even luck out and find glow-in-the-dark solar systems for ceilings or see-through models of circulatory systems and auto engines for shelves.

Seasonal decorations: Decorations create teaching moments, whether posters of the Bay Colony at Thanksgiving, the Via Dolorosa at Easter, or the manger scene at Christmas. Flags and patriotic banners at Veterans Day, D-Day, and presidents' birthdays are great, and they even allow for surreptitious summer learning on Memorial Day and July Fourth. Wonderful faux parchment reproductions of the Declaration of Independence are available in catalogs too.

Relishing the thought of surprising her at lunch, I slipped into the cafeteria with a chocolate shake in my hand. A mother of six, I don't get many chances to impulsively sweeten my kids' days, so it was as much a gift to myself as it was to my 11-year-old.

I found my middle daughter alone at a table, spearing Tater Tots with her fork.

She stared at the gymnasium wall, trying hard to ignore a table nearby full of giggling, flirty classmates who had no trouble ignoring her.

My heart broke.

Slated to enter junior high that next fall, there was no way this child would be ready.

She had always been a loner. Now, in fifth grade, her peers began to notice her quirks. Next year, in full hormonal reign, they would chew her up and spit her out. Sex, drugs and criminal activities all seem viable options to a child who feels these things might gain them social acceptance. I'd do anything to keep my daughter from ever considering those choices.

Dear God, I thought, *You'll have to help me. I'm going to have to homeschool her.*

Doubts immediately arose.

My patience level often resembles a short fuse on a stick of dynamite. I couldn't teach the math that I never fully understood myself. And might not the insularity of homeschool just make my daughter more delayed in her social development?

A few minor issues aside, we've been happy with our area schools. Small town, approachable administrators and communicative teachers all combined to create an atmosphere that fostered positive relationships between families and the education district.

But we know several couples who homeschool due to the public schools' lack of morals and their teaching of evolution. Other kids are just too bright or too bored to be in regular classrooms. Some use home education to encourage non-academic interests such as music or art.

People like me just want to let their kids be kids until it's time to move on. In their own time, not society's.

I knew my friends would help me put together a solid curriculum, and I'd get to fill the gaps I'd noticed in my daughter's education.

But could I give up a big part of my day on a regular basis? I wasn't sure. What about family prejudice? When my brother and his wife chose to homeschool they were told they were "making that child a social outcast." And was I strong enough to face the stares and assumptions triggered by a 12-year-old at the mall on a school day?

My daughter still attends band, math and choral classes at her local junior high, which has been surprisingly supportive. When the naysayers screech out warnings about isolation and socialization skills, I can point to the field trips and parties; drug education and game days at her after-school program.

To be honest, I miss my freedom terribly and I hate grading papers. I'm a washout at Science experiments, and sometimes resent the money homeschool materials cost me. My daughter misses the school assemblies, the theme days and the pure silliness of girls her age.

But our gains have eclipsed our losses. I no longer feel guilty that my child suffers at the hands of her unkind peers. Free from the stress of hunting for a slot to fit into, she's changing local educators' opinions about their role in today's homeschool movement.

In return for my sacrifice, I've regained a child with a happy heart.[7]

Teaching a heart to be happy certainly would not qualify as academics. But lessons in self-assurance are part of those we must administer, even when a detour from traditional subjects is required. Her daughter has returned to public schools now, but Sheila knows she made the right decision to pull her out when she did.

"I've had many former doubters comment that she's such a happy girl now and admit to me that I did the

93

right thing," Sheila says. "Many parents tell me they so wish they'd been more aggressive about considering other options for their own kids. While I still don't feel part of the homeschool loop, and mine wasn't an all-out venture, it proved a lifesaver! I'm no longer afraid of homeschooling, and I'll do it again if need be. After all, I do have three more kids, and so much damage can occur during those junior high years."[8]

Don't Board Up Your Window of Opportunity

You have yet another advantage as parent/teacher: a running, jumping, double-twist, freestyle-combination head start. But in order to keep that edge, you have to stay on top of your game and remember you're in training. It's easy to lose your advantage through negligence or oversight. Or simply because you don't recognize the advantage is there.

If you hold back because you're certain your kids are too young to learn, you're just throwing precious time away. Studies have shown that from the moment of birth, infants recognize their mother's voice and the voices of those who have been constantly around her. That kind of instant recognition isn't instinctive; it's a learned response to nine months of outside input.

In other words, the doctor only put a stethoscope to your belly at monthly intervals, but that kid had the earphones on 24/7. Listening. Being naturally nosey.

If he's two minutes old, your potential for input just increased dramatically.

The absorption level of children up to age five is staggering. When you compare the vocabulary base of a three-year-old to that of a kid finishing grade school and find it hasn't expanded all that much, it can even be discouraging. And that's just by measuring formal academic input. What about all the things toddlers learn about family relationships, the world around them, hot and cold, high and low, how the dog's tongue feels on their faces, and what the goldfish tastes like? The crux of the matter isn't whether they can handle it so young but whether we're too lazy or preoccupied with tasks like feeding and burping them to build their academic base.

"Somehow, the age of 6 became the American age at which formal education is begun, the so-called age of readiness," say the Engelmanns. "It is certainly much easier to communicate with a child of 6, and they will be easier to teach. Better yet, why not wait until the child is 10 or 14? But the gains that a child achieves during the preschool years give him a real head start. If the child who receives early instruction has mastered more skills by the age of 6 than the average 6-year-old, he is ahead in two ways: he knows more and is capable of learning additional skills more rapidly."[9]

Ability to Conquer Disabilities

Great. So we've cornered the market on input before age six, the best and most effective input. We're all geared up and psyched up. We hit the ground running and have a great plan and a fine array of quality educational materials. Our hands are in God's hands, and our kids' hands are in ours. The future seems bright—till we discover that a child in our home has a disability.

What can a parent do about those children who have real, verifiable educational challenges? How can you, a nonexpert without a degree in special ed, hope to properly teach this child? What if you don't know how to begin to find his or her learning style?

In a previous chapter we talked about not letting the system slap a "disability" label on your kids, and by and large, this holds true. But the fact is that certain children do have genuine disabilities. These kids must receive a more targeted effort in order to help them succeed.

This is a hurdle, to be sure. But homeschool offers you a chance to grab one hand while God grabs the other, and together you can help that child leap over the hurdle.

The good news is that parents have an edge here too in that they can usually identify and address the problem at a very early age, thus laying the groundwork for a successful academic career. They can perceive a child's weaknesses, find emerging habit patterns, and learn how to interact with the child in a beneficial way. They can spark academic intrigue based on the child's personality, talents, and interests. They can practice dealing with any deficiencies before formal education begins. Once begun, they can proceed at a pace that the child finds workable without the pressure of having him keep up with the class.

But sometimes such an early opportunity isn't available, as in the case of later adoption.

What then?

Alan and Dana Mihalko faced just such a scenario. They've taken their share of negative criticism on their choice to homeschool all three of their children, but specifically their adopted daughter, Mary.

The Mihalkos are a military family. Dana is a self-proclaimed "military brat" who met her husband while working in a beauty salon in Georgia, where they were both saved and married. They were stationed in New Mexico and Arizona and had two sons before moving to Mississippi, where their chance came to adopt a little girl.

"The adoption agency gave us a book of kids with disabilities," says Dana. "I think they try to present the needier kids to couples who already have children, and that's probably a good thing."

They spent time looking through the choices and studying each child's background. Mary seemed to fit them just right.

"It wasn't because she was a particularly pretty child," Dana says. "The picture in the book was just awful, and the caseworkers told us about all the things that could possibly go wrong. I know it was just God."

At ten, Mary would be their oldest child. She was mildly mentally retarded, a condition that slowed her reasoning skills. Justin had been homeschooled a little in their travels, but at seven he was a bit behind in reading. Daniel, at four, was ready to start learning to read. Dana decided to teach them all together and keep them at the same grade level.

Family members freely offered the opinion that Alan and Dana's decision to homeschool would prove disastrous. But the Mihalkos credit homeschooling with bringing about a quick and strong bond with Mary. They were able to spend many hours together each day and became comfortable with each other in a hurry.

Math was a particularly challenging subject for Mary because it's a discipline built on previous knowledge, which would sometimes escape her.

"There were times when I thought, *She'll never get this,* and it would take her such a long time," her mother says. "But she's so diligent. If she were to be scored on diligence alone, she'd be an *A*+ student. When I tell her it's time for a break she'll say, 'Wait. I need to finish this first,' and she won't let up till it's done."

Dana found praise to be a wonderful tool in homeschooling her disabled daughter.

"It seemed more valuable to praise her for her effort than to award her a low grade," she says. "I told her how well she was doing and that she just needed to fix these certain things. When she came back with the corrections, I gave her a good grade."

97

After all, don't we all need encouragement?

Ten years later, all three children are finishing high school. Justin, seventeen, wants to pursue a career as an electrician. Daniel, fifteen, has aspirations to become an actor or singer, although his parents are encouraging other possible choices. At twenty, Mary is a high school senior with a solid *C* average despite her disability.

Dana's secret weapon was prayer. Coupled with persistence, it's reaped an effective testimony.

"It's spoken volumes to our family members," says Dana. "At first they panicked and didn't think I could do it—and I couldn't have without God! Now, they're full of applause."[10]

Back in Action

One more social twist on the advantages of home education lies in the fact that Dad too is able to influence the kids. "One of the most sacred cows of our culture, the American public school, has had tremendously negative effects on the masculinity of the males of our society," says Weldon Hardenbrook, author of *Missing from Action: Vanishing Manhood in America.* "Only father-absence exerts a greater feminizing influence on our boys than do the schools of our land."[11]

It's worthy of note that Hardenbrook's wife taught public school for years, so he speaks from a base of personal experience.

Think of the hours upon hours that your children spend being henpecked by teachers, coaches, and the school nurse. As soon as their feet hit the front step, it's Mom's turn: "Did you feed the dog? Did you study your math? Did you practice your horn? Can you feed the baby while I make dinner? I'm swamped!" Dad arrives, takes stock of the cereal-covered toddler and his frazzled wife and seeks refuge in the bathroom with the latest *Reader's Digest*. At dinner the pleasantries are limited to "Pass the salt" and "How was your day?" When nobody's home, family ties all but disappear as each member pursues separate interests.

Homeschool families have the advantage of a closer-knit clan. The seven to twelve hours spent away from home for educational purposes have been bought back, affording family members the privilege of remembering each other's names. Dad may still work outside the home, but when he arrives, everyone is excited to join in telling him what went on all day, because the day was a shared experience, and the school in his home is exciting to him. Family outings and trips can be scheduled when Dad is free, regardless of the day, week, or month. Memories are built together at home and abroad, and he's a real part of them.

The family monarch has his proper place as the authority to which all appeals are made. He's the study hall tutor, the principal, and the good guy who can call unexpected afternoons off when he gets home early.

Dad's also the shepherd of his flock. It's up to him to minister to his congregation at home and see them grow in grace. R. C. Sproul Jr., who with wife Denise homeschools his own six, reminds us to render unto Caesar the things that are Caesar's but unto God the things that are God's. "Our children are a heritage from the Lord," says Sproul, "and [we're] refusing to render unto Caesar that which bears God's image."[12]

For those dads who have exercised the right to be part of their children's education, the rewards can be very satisfying.

"Teaching Shiloh has been one of the most fulfilling things I've ever done in my life," says Bill Tinsley.

Here's a man who runs his own business and ministers in his home church. Yet homeschooling his daughter was an experience he counts among his life's most fulfilling.

Bill and his wife, Donna, live in Florida with their four daughters. They began teaching the youngest at home when she was nine years old.

"After four frustrating years of public education, we realized the school was not meeting the need of our dyslexic daughter," says Donna. "After much prayer, we felt homeschooling was the answer. But my lack of formal education made me feel insecure about doing it myself."

Bill had no teaching credentials and, being self-employed, couldn't afford time off from work to homeschool. Nevertheless, he felt God gifting him for the job and was eager to begin. Rising at 4:00 A.M., he'd do paperwork, then leave by 6:00 to pick up materials and deliver them to his crew. He'd return by 8:00 to work with Shiloh for several hours before heading back to work. Donna helped with home economics and set up field trips with a local homeschool group.

"When my homeschooling friends came over, I was more than a little jealous," Donna says. "Suddenly they had a lot more to say to Bill than to me: What are you using for math? This worked best for us, and so on."

As for Bill, he often felt like a juggler spinning multiple stacks of plates.

"But he taught with such grace," says Donna. "I would often hear them laughing as Bill explained math concepts to her. In our hectic world, I saw something precious: a father spending time with his daughter."

Business grew and work demanded more time. The Tinsleys began a home renovation project, and it became evident that homeschooling would be too much on Bill's plate. Donna felt the Lord nudging her to look to him as her source and take over schooling Shiloh.

"I believe we overcome by the blood of the Lamb and the word of our testimony," she says. "We have a possible

100

trip planned to North Carolina, Tennessee, and Louisiana, which will be quite an experience, since neither Shiloh nor I have ever been on an airplane."[13]

Luci Shaw says, "Whether we are poets or parents or teachers or artists or gardeners, we must start where we are and use what we have. In the process of creation and relationship, what seems mundane and trivial may show itself to be holy; precious; part of a pattern."[14]

When things slow down for him, Bill Tinsley plans to teach his daughter again. Because once you taste something that brings meaning to life, it's hard to let it go.

Lifesavers

1. God doesn't want his people to follow the educational fads of the world just because they're popular. He wants us to have the edge and be a class above. He intends that his people prepare themselves to be the pacesetters and the cream that rises to the top and shows others how it's done:

And the LORD will make you the head and not the tail; you shall be above only, and not beneath, if you heed the commandments of the LORD your God, which I command you today, and are careful to observe them.

Deuteronomy 28:13

A wise man scales the city of the mighty,
And brings down the trusted stronghold.

Proverbs 21:22

101

> The lips of the righteous feed many,
> But fools die for lack of wisdom.
>
> Proverbs 10:21

> He who troubles his own house will inherit the
> wind,
> And the fool will be servant to the wise of heart.
>
> Proverbs 11:29

2. Never forget to make use of your great homeschool advantages. Our kids have been given to us so we can present them back to their heavenly Father. His image is stamped upon them, and it's up to us at home to teach them from his Word about their godly heritage and calling—to birth in them a love of him and show them the more excellent way.

And He said to them, "Whose image and inscription is this?"
They said to Him, "Caesar's."
And He said to them, "Render therefore to Caesar the things that are Caesar's, and to God the things that are God's."

Matthew 22:20

As you know how we exhorted, and comforted, and charged every one of you, as a father does his own children, that you would walk worthy of God who calls you into His own kingdom and glory.

1 Thessalonians 2:11–12

And that from childhood you have known the Holy Scriptures, which are able to make you wise for salvation through faith which is in Jesus Christ.

2 Timothy 3:15

3. Our advantage in home education includes teaching our children what the real wisdom is: the fear of

the Lord. In doing so, we can train them to develop wise hearts, hearts that seek God and so find true and eternal understanding. When we release them at last from home education, their hearts will know a better way, and they can show others where true wisdom lies. And as worldly philosophies arise and wag their tongues against the truth, they'll know nothing can stand against God's Word.

The heart of the prudent acquires knowledge,
And the ear of the wise seeks knowledge.

Proverbs 18:15

Understanding is a wellspring of life to him
    who has it,
But the correction of fools is folly.
The heart of the wise teaches his mouth,
And adds learning to his lips.

Proverbs 16:22–23

Give instruction to a wise man, and he will be still
    wiser;
Teach a just man, and he will increase in learning.
The fear of the LORD is the beginning of wisdom,
And the knowledge of the Holy One is understanding.

Proverbs 9:9–10

Those who are wise shall shine
Like the brightness of the firmament,
And those who turn many to righteousness
Like the stars forever and ever.

Daniel 12:3

There is no wisdom or understanding
Or counsel against the LORD.

Proverbs 21:30

5

Education Is More than Academics

Clean Brains Are Healthy Brains

Of all the parts of kids that need washing, their brains need it the most. Overpaid athletes, shallow models, Hollywood stars, even their favorite TV friends—all take turns brainwashing your children. An innocent-looking TV commercial has the power to send them into paroxysms of rage if you don't buy the toy of the month.

But before you blame them for this Pavlovian response, ask yourself, How many toys have *I* been sold this month?

Madison Avenue preys upon a fact that educators have known for years: Repetition is a highly effective method for burning stuff into gray matter. This is why, in the course of a two-hour TV movie, you'll get sold the same

SUV six times. It would be so much more entertaining if it was sold six different ways, but that's not the marketers' goal. They only care that by the time the movie credits roll, you can repeat their commercial verbatim.

And have you purged from your brain any of those jingles that you heard as a five-year-old? If you're old enough, you probably still know exactly how far you'd walk for a Camel, why my dog is better than your dog, and why you wish you were an Oscar Mayer wiener.

Pretty scary, huh? But take heart: The same technique works for teaching your child ABCs and church songs. And a theory called the Mozart Effect says that a kid who grows up listening to classical music will develop an aptitude and love for it. Not to mention a natural sense of rhythm, logic, and math. Wow! That's a pretty good return for such a small investment.

Speaking of sales pitches, remember that books are media too. They carry an agenda and a message. Never underestimate the power of words—read or heard. And hey, Mom, some of the best personal reading time—perhaps the *only* reading time—that you'll get in your parenting career is during nursing sessions. Think about it: You can sit down in one spot and relax, feed, and read. Why not read your book of the month out loud and let "Spongy Pie" soak it all in?

Just make sure it's worthwhile material. While you may think she's still too young, everything that's read out loud to this kid is being soaked up along with the milk and is bound to influence her. So be selective about her books even before she's reading them herself. Keep the quality level high, and above all, be sure you both have fun when you read to her. Reading should always be a positive experience.

As authors go, Dr. Seuss is—hands down—our biggest hero. Reading was beginning to look mighty grim before Puff and Spot got the heave-ho in deference to Thing One and Thing Two. Seuss books offer the most fun allowable by law, especially if the reader is well practiced in Seussian cadence and reads nonsense with the twinkle in which it was written. Dr. Seuss, like Chuck Jones, wrote for adults. The older you get, the more you enjoy Bugs Bunny's sarcasm and the Cat in the Hat's one-liners. When you sit down with your kids to watch Bugs or read the Cat, you can be sure at least one person will always get something out of it: you.

Your kids will learn something too—that you're genuinely enjoying time with them and that reading is a blast. Most of all, the children learn that you care about spending time with them, so it follows that they must be worth caring about. They learn that they're important. That they matter. That they're loved. Later they'll learn that even God thought they were worth loving and saving. What's more important than that?

This is more than a reading lesson. It's a love-of-reading lesson.

Fitzhugh Mullan served the U.S. Public Health Service for twenty years as a policy maker and then returned to private practice in Washington, D.C., where he now sees underprivileged children every day. In his March 2000 article "Rx for Reading," he links slow speech to lack of reading with the parent:

> Books are rare commodities in the homes of my patients. When I make house calls, televisions are omnipresent and turned on. There are toys, but I rarely see any books. Poverty, often complicated by language barriers, puts children's books way down on the priority list of many families in my practice. Speech problems and language delays trouble many of our young patients. Researchers and educators have shown that early experiences with books are critically linked to a child's success in learning to read. Even picture books for toddlers grab the mind, stimulate language and excite the imagination.

Books invite a parent and child to sit down together, to snuggle, to talk and think together. In the process, parents teach language and values, show affection and have a good time.[1]

Libraries are fabulous places but often underrated and overlooked. Tome after tome may be accessed on virtually any subject in the world, and books of pure nonsense can aerate and reconstitute a child's fried brain cells after an intensive day of homeschool. The amount of academic output you can squeeze out of a kid with the promise of an outing to these halls of wisdom is simply staggering.

My husband has learned how to fix virtually everything—from Studebakers to air conditioning units—from books. These days hardbacks have given way to software: Timeless classics can be ingested on a library cassette or CD; in-home classrooms can be created via borrowed VHS or DVD. We've checked out computer software tutorials, Shakespearean plays, American classics, presidential biographies, and visual world geography lessons on video. We've taken advantage of video workshops on everything from home repair to cake decorating to tap dancing.

I admired my oldest daughter's display of coffee-table books the other day. Then I picked one up and found a library tag on the spine. On closer examination I found they all had tags.

"Don't you just love the library?" said Dina, who had been remodeling her home a room at a time. Books on paint, cabinetry, and color schemes were the pick of the week at her house. Her sisters have checked out books on puppet fabrication and tailoring. Her brothers gravitate to those on car repair and rocket engines. Nevertheless, they all fall under the category of surreptitious study, explained à la Mark Twain:

107

If he [Tom Sawyer] had been a great and wise philoso-
pher, like the writer of this book, he would now have
comprehended that Work consists of whatever a body
is obliged to do, and Play consists of whatever a body is
not obliged to do. And this would help him understand
why constructing artificial flowers or performing on a
treadmill is work, while rolling tenpins or climbing Mont
Blanc is only amusement.[2]

Lessons are only work when they're packaged and
announced, but if you're sharp and find new venues,
learning can happen all the time—especially for culti-
vated bookworms. This species is nurtured and aerated
in the rich humus of the written page, and shelves upon
shelves of these pages, not to mention tapes and DVDs,
reside at your local public library.

Make it a regular habit to go there, and make it a
memorable time with the kids so that they'll look forward to it with anticipation. We had to institute library
rules: No reading books at the library that Mama hasn't
approved. No checking out books that Mama hasn't approved. Only five library books per kid during the school
term, and seven per kid during the summer. (Remember,
we had eight kids: you do the math). No reading books
on the way home in the car. No reading books till they're
catalogued on the computer at home and released to
you. All library books must be kept in the library box
so they don't get lost. No touching library books with
dirty hands or while eating. No taking library books
into bedrooms at night.

After all, in a three-week checkout period, these books
become part of the family. There have to be some boundaries or the librarian will never see them again or be able
to recognize them. They can be well loved as long as it's
not too obvious. And we do want them to be loved.

Kids who struggle with reading are those who see no point in it. They've never seen reading as an enjoyable pastime because nobody ever took the time to make it memorable. Time, like money, is *you* in spendable form. Even half an hour can be golden when you consider the lifelong love affair you'll cultivate between your kids and books and the closeness you'll build together in special moments and shared memories. After that, books are no longer a chore but a door of opportunity to be unlocked on virtually any subject. And books afford yet another venue for early input.

Your potential for early input as a parent is overwhelming when you realize your exclusive access begins way before they're born. No, I don't discount the impact of prenatal input. Been there. Done that. Wore out the headphones.

Did it help? Who knows? But it couldn't hurt!

So are we maximizing all this early potential or letting it slip through our overinvolved fingers? While we're too busy with life beyond the crib to appreciate what's right under our noses, the world sets up our kids' internal programming, flops on the couch with the popcorn, and makes ready to click their remotes.

Parents must win the brainwashing race. We are duty and honor bound to get there before the world does and to wash in the good stuff—values, convictions, love of God, morals, work ethic, patriotism, loyalty, responsibility, maturity. You know, all that great stuff that used to be taught at school.

Raising a Brilliant Human

So many cleaning products! So little time! What crucial items do we impart? What ingredients make an educated adult? Now, there's a debate that still rages at the top of today's news, as the traditional ways to measure intelligence are weighed and found wanting. Do you know what they've discovered? That you can't extract a kid from her home environment for ten to twelve hours a day of school, extracurricular activities, and/or day care and still expect that she'll become a functional adult on the merits of book learning alone.

Self-discipline, responsibility, business before pleasure, putting others first, and all that other great advice your mother gave you are the cornerstones of success in life as a human being. If we can instill these gems and at the same time impart a love of discovery that will take a child beyond our own personal knowledge, we've produced a lifelong learner.

Montessori says a child's work is his preparation for life. In other words, teaching happens at the same time life happens. The jobs we think of as boring—washing dishes, feeding the dog, and peeling potatoes—are exciting to kids because it gives them the chance to imitate adults. Until it becomes their regular chore; then it's a job you should have relegated to a sibling. So enjoy the early learning aura while it lasts, and when they begin to complain, tell them they're developing intellectually, physically, socially, and creatively.

Someday they'll thank you, but it may be a while.

Many kinds of intelligence can be demonstrated in a variety of ways, some of which can't be clinically measured. Some Ph.D.s who can split atoms with half a brain tied behind their backs are incredibly dumb about such mundane challenges as communicating with their wives and remembering their children's birthdays.

Now, I ask you: Which of these skills are they likely to use more often?

Education is about the whole child as a person, not about some hyperintelligent, oversized brains controlling the world from isolation chambers like an old *Star Trek* episode.

Helen Keller said that children will educate themselves under the right circumstances. Parents *can* teach a child to learn how to learn, to enjoy learning as a lifelong adventure. It's informal learning, or what Montessori called the directive environment. It's learning on the hoof, using everything around us in order to acquire knowledge.

Basic principles of real life aren't taught on the blackboard. Learning isn't only about information that we label as knowledge. Learning is something we do. It's the kind of thinking that moves us forward in our search for understanding. It's knowledge in all areas, acquired over the course of a lifetime. It's seizing the moment in the course of a normal day to say or do something to deepen a child's thinking or put her in touch with her own feelings and direct her to pursue worthy goals, personal skills, creativity, or talents.

While life is happening, we're transmitting knowledge, wisdom, experience, culture, traditions, beliefs—in short, who we are and what we know—to the next generation.

Academics are part of this, to be sure. But while we focus on deliberate input, let's not neglect nontraditional subjects like, for instance, real home economics. Economics of the home, that is. Budgeting and living within your means so that your car and your house don't wind up getting repossessed. Paying your bills on time. Saving for a worthwhile goal instead of getting into debt for it. Calculating what you can actually afford *before* you spend it. Wow! What a concept! Who teaches this stuff? If it was taught, we wouldn't be such a credit-dependent society.

Simply learning to live in a civilized fashion with one's siblings can develop leadership and people skills that will stand a child in good stead in his future workplace. There wouldn't be a need for all those crisis and anger management seminars and therapists at a zillion bucks an hour if kids were brought up with a few simple principles, such as: No, you may not use your sister's baby doll as a basketball—even if it does make that great *swoosh* going through the hoop—because it hurts your sister's feelings. Just because the game is fun for you doesn't make it fun for everybody. It only qualifies for fun if everyone enjoys it.

But what about your child's fragile self-image? Many educators say if you impose any form of discipline or let on that he's not the center of the universe, you'll give your child a complex and destroy his self-image. To be perfectly honest, the real self-image crisis isn't about who our kids are. It's about who they aren't—and who God says they are.

They're not born to be puppets of a worldly pseudo-intellectualism fueled by a humanistic mind-set. They're born to be lights for God in this crooked, perverse, "whatever" generation. Don't abdicate your position of influence and withhold your input because the "committee of they" says it's unfair for you to influence their decisions. Trust me: If you listen to the "committee," you'll be the only one who doesn't influence your children. We can't just let them stumble out there and become part of the darkness when they're called to be the light of the world (Matt. 5:14–16).

Last, but certainly not least, remember that education includes and is keyed to the simple awakening of a healthy, natural, human curiosity that will continue to beckon your children into an ever-expanding world of wonder and knowledge. In short, the "ooh and aah factor."

The Swallow's Nest on the Altar

Sounds like a cool CD title, doesn't it? Well, it *was* a song. In Psalm 84:3: "Even . . . the swallow [has found]

Field Trips: You're Walking on a Gold Mine

Get curious! Grab the Yellow Pages! Many places offer free school tours:

- Museums, planetariums, observatories, or airstrips
- Aquarium, wildlife preserve, or zoo docent tours
- Camp or hike national forests or natural landmarks
- Historical landmarks, battlefields, or reenactments
- Dairy farm, cattle ranch, flower growers, or riding stables*
- Back-room tour of supermarket, florist, print shop, or machine shop
- Taxidermists, candle makers, glassblowers, potters, or graphic artists
- Newspaper office, TV station, radio station, or Western Union
- Post office, police station, fire station, or military base
- Local team's spring training or theater's dress rehearsals
- Park concerts/drama "under the stars" (and picnic dinner)

*Choose whatever's unique to your area. We have an ostrich farm nearby!

a nest for herself, where she may lay her young—even Your altars, O LORD of hosts."

Now there's a wise old bird. That shows us something pretty significant about mama swallow: She was so at home in the house of God and so used to spending time with him at the altar, that it was the most natural place in the world to build her nest and raise her babies.

And there lies the single most valuable benefit of running your Christian homeschool: The kids grow up at the altar with their parents. Praying with them; worshiping with them; having family devotions, Bible lessons, and creation science lessons with them. In short, learning their faith, which is a lost freedom in the public school world. If you relinquish your kids to the system, they'll be taught every faith but yours. Talk about discrimination! In our overly tolerant, nonjudgmental society where nothing is ever really "wrong," godliness is the only taboo.

"From the start government schools were designed to create pliable, obedient servants of industry and the state," says R. C. Sproul Jr. "That means that they must teach the children the religion of the state. It means they must seek to sever the ties of kinship. You, Mom and Dad, are in the way."[3]

Our right to bring kids up in our own faith is quickly vanishing as we succumb to discrimination masquerading as political correctness. In the world of public education, Christians have lost both their freedom of speech and their freedom of religion in the name of cultural and religious tolerance.

But this really isn't about culture or religion. This is about the world kicking God off the throne in deference to man. Christianity teaches that Jesus can't be kicked off the throne and declares him to be the only way. Therefore, *Christianity* alone remains as a dirty word in our anything-goes society.

But let me ask you a hard question: Who's demonstrating the alternative to these kids? You're their teacher now. That's great. Will you take the responsibility to show your child a superior faith? The Bible says, "Oh, taste and see that the LORD is good" (Ps. 34:8). So who's handing out taste samples and doing demonstrations? It had better be you. Will you nest those cute little baby birds on God's altar and poke good-tasting things into their wide-open beaks? Remember those little people are only yours on loan. They're given to you so you can give them back to God. That means you must show them the way to him.

Have you caught their interest enough that they'll go with you? Would they want to know God as you know him? Do you show them by your own example how to hit the altar daily and repent of sin, to remain there and become a living sacrifice (Rom. 12:1–2), giving your life up to him, consciously giving the steering wheel back to God? Whether we're aware of it or not, for good or ill, we're our kids' primary example in prayer, zeal, and a personal walk with God. That means it falls to us to help them establish godly habits. To teach them how to cultivate a habit of personal daily devotions.

Cleanliness is next to godliness, your grandma always told you. That means Bible reading and prayer should be happening right along with face washing and toothbrushing, trained into your kids as a regular part of morning activities never to be neglected. You wouldn't let your kid get by with dragon breath, and you shouldn't let him go without brushing his spiritual teeth either. You don't want cobwebs on his Bible any more than you do on his toothbrush. Personal habits established in childhood stay with us for life. Be sure Bible reading and prayer are two of them, and you will have given your child a gift that will help him find God as his personal friend.

We must have deliberate spiritual input with our kids. If not us, who?

Let's start at the beginning: The names we give our children are our first chance to speak blessing into their lives. In the Bible, names were given as prophecies to be fulfilled. Aspirations to achieve. Blessings to grab hold of.

Read some of the meanings of biblical names: Man of God (Gabriel); Source of Joy (Abigail); Crowned (Stephen); Vindication/Justice (Dinah); Gift of God (Nathanael); Son of the Right Hand (Benjamin); Favored (Anna); Heard of God (Samuel); Favored of Jehovah (John, Joanna).[4] Wow! Pretty cool stuff, really!

They're born, and then what happens? They throw the cat in the dryer, use the ketchup for finger paint, and shave their little sister's head bald playing barber. Hey, they're kids, remember? Not short adults. Teach them what their names mean and encourage them to do great things in God. Don't stop speaking those blessings, even if it *is* through gritted teeth. "Death and life are in the power of the tongue" (Prov. 18:21), and although sometimes we wish it were that easy, we do want to remember to speak blessing and not cursing, encouragement and not discouragement. Have patience. God will give it to you as surely as he'll bless and enlighten your children's understanding. While often neither feels certain, one can be the product of the other. Desperation is also the mother of invention.

In our personal quest for deliberate programming, we found an ally in modern technology. You've heard of people learning foreign languages by listening to tapes while they fall asleep? Well, we tried the tape thing with Scriptures and Bible stories and church songs, as well as with ABCs and counting exercises. Sticking a tape player halfway down the hall between the bedroom doors, we figured our little angels would absorb everything into their subconscious psyches while they peacefully dozed off. It sounded like a perfect plan. There was just one drawback: Nobody fell asleep. It wasn't supposed to be part of the program for the kids to holler down the hall for Mom and Dad to flip the tape over.

Twice.

But twenty-five years later, every one of them can still tell you those stories and sing every song. And twenty-five years later, they all still love and serve God. So do their kids. And they're all getting their socks blessed off on a regular basis because God's their loving Dad.

Guess the falling asleep part wasn't as vital as we thought.

Still, this isn't the golden key that gets you off the hook. You can't just put your kids on autopilot via tapes and books. These are great supplemental tools, to be sure, but you must be there for them personally as well. Live and in color. Up close and personal. You. Mom and Dad.

In teaching our faith to our children, few things are as crucial as the family altar, with the accent on family. Together. Carving out a few sacred moments before bedtime, at the end of the day, to recap and recoup, to braid up all the fraying loose ends, and to look to God together. This is Dad's moment to give spiritual input as the head of the house. Mornings often fall to Mom, as Dad's generally gone before the short people's patrol comes on duty. But at night we must prop eyelids open with toothpicks and find those extra moments to turn to God, thank him for everything, and lay requests before him as a family.

He won't be Lord later if we don't crown him now.

Reality Check

Homeschooler Tina Lewis found out early that schools aren't necessarily about academic learning anymore, and that parental input is an imperative:

One day when my son Eric was in kindergarten, he brought home a book from the school library with a skull and cross bones on the cover. The book was about celebrating what

117

happens after death and was totally against my beliefs and a few years above his grade level. I fought to get it out of the school but it stayed in the name of "culture."

But, where's God? Not in the schools anymore, I think.

I made sure the principal knew there were no books about Jesus Christ in that library.

Upon visiting the classroom one day I discovered that the first thing they did was to sit everybody in a circle and ask how they felt. To me this is clearly a push for the liberal agenda that says your feelings control your life and are more important than academics; more important than right or wrong; more important than God.

At six years old, Eric would go off to school and come home with a chip on his shoulder. During vacations I had my good little boy back within a couple of days—until he returned to school and the bad attitude returned to his life. I began to worry about his eternal future.

I hadn't finished my quiet time with God one morning when I put Eric on the bus and the strong feeling hit me as it had at other times: I was sending him to a place he shouldn't be. I've been homeschooling for two years now and have no doubt it's God's will. Within our first month Eric said to me, "Thank you that I'm learning about God and the Bible all day."

Most things that are worthwhile aren't easy. There are times when it's challenging, but the blessings and peace outweigh the negatives a hundredfold.[5]

Parents are increasingly alarmed at the lack of academics in our academies. The three R's are woefully absent in today's politically correct schools that are far more concerned that children be self-aware than literate. But it's a universal truth that children are aware of little else. Of today's alternative curricula Sykes notes, "Children who emerge from twelve years or more of such courses may or may not have a healthy 'self-concept,' but it seems possible that they will also be self-satisfied egotists."[6]

Beyond the fact that schools no longer steep kids in pure academics, and beyond the fact that nonessential curricula bear no resemblance to what you want your kids programmed with, consider another reality check: Are your children being prepared to face real life as we know it?

Schools as we know them today don't prepare kids for the real world. Not as free thinkers, at any rate. Charles J. Sykes, author of *Dumbing Down Our Kids: Why American Children Feel Good About Themselves But Can't Read, Write, or Add,* gives some wonderfully down-to-earth advice about life lessons that schools don't teach. He exposes the prevalent feel-good-about-you, life-is-your-oyster, you're-always-right-so-blame-everyone-else-if-you-can't-cut-it, politically correct, culturally tolerant, quasieducational system that is not based in reality, thus setting kids up for failure in the real world. "The square root of 99 is still 9.498743," he says, "no matter how a child feels about it."[7]

Here are Sykes's rules for real life beyond the classroom:

1. *Life is not fair. Get used to it.* The average teenager uses the phrase "it's not fair" 8.6 times a day. The kids got it from their parents who said it so often they decided they must be the most idealistic generation ever. When the parents started hearing it from their own kids, they realized rule #1.
2. *The real world won't care as much as your school does about your self-esteem.* It'll expect you to accomplish something before you feel good about yourself. This may come as a shock. When inflated self-esteem meets reality most kids complain that it's not fair. (See rule #1.)
3. *Sorry, you won't make $40,000 a year right out of high school.* And you won't be a vice president or have a car phone either. You may even have to wear a uniform that doesn't have a GAP label.

4. *If you think your teacher is tough, wait till you get a boss.* He doesn't have tenure, so he tends to be a bit edgier. When you screw up, he's not going to ask you how you feel about it.

5. *Your school may have done away with winners and losers. Life hasn't.* In some schools, they'll give you as many times as you want to get the right answer. Failing grades have been abolished and class valedictorians scrapped, lest anyone's feelings be hurt. Effort is as important as results. This, of course, bears not the slightest resemblance to anything in real life. See rules #1, 2, and 4.

6. *Flipping burgers is not beneath your dignity.* Your grandparents had a different word for burger flipping. They called it opportunity. They weren't embarrassed making minimum wage either. They would have been embarrassed to sit around talking about Kurt Cobain all weekend.

7. *Television is not real life.* Your life is not a sitcom. Your problems will not all be solved in thirty minutes, minus time for commercials. In real life people actually have to leave the coffee shop to go to jobs. Your friends will not be perky, sexy, or predictable as Jennifer Aniston.

8. *Before you were born your parents weren't as boring as they are now.* They got that way paying your bills, cleaning up your room and listening to you tell them how idealistic you are. And by the way, before you save the rain forest from the blood sucking parasites of your parents' generation, try delousing the closet in your bedroom.

9. *Life is not divided into semesters. And you don't get summers off.* Not even Easter break. They expect you to show up every day. For 8 hours. And you don't get a new life every 10 weeks. It just goes on and on. While we're at it, few jobs are interested in fostering your self-expression or helping you find yourself. Fewer still lead to self-realization. See rules #1 and 2.

10. *It's not your parents' fault. If you screw up, you are responsible.* This is the flip side of "It's my life," and "You're not the boss of me," and other eloquent proclamations of your generation. When you turn 18, it's on your dime. Don't whine about it or you'll sound like a baby boomer.

11. *Be nice to nerds. You may end up working for them. We all could.*

12. *Smoking doesn't make you look cool. It makes you look moronic.* Next time you're out cruising, watch an 11-year-old with a butt in his mouth. That's what you look like to anyone over 20. Ditto for "expressing yourself" with purple hair and/or pierced body parts.

13. *You are not immortal.* See rule #9. If you are under the impression that living fast, dying young, and leaving a beautiful corpse is romantic, you obviously haven't seen one of your peers at room temperature lately.

14. *Enjoy this while you can.* Sure parents are a pain, school's a bother, and life is depressing. Someday you'll realize how wonderful it was to be a kid. Maybe you should start now.[8]

Thinking men have strong opinions about the relativity of what's taught in traditional classrooms. Albert Einstein said, "It is nothing short of a miracle that modern methods of instruction have not yet entirely strangled the holy curiosity of inquiry. *Education is that which remains when one has forgotten everything learned in school*" (emphasis added).[9]

Duty, Honor, and Other Taboos

All academics are part of an education, but an education isn't all about academics.

The school of hard knocks will also give you an education. That's where you learn the important stuff, such as: The hardness of the butter is directly proportional to the softness of the bread; and the colder the X-ray table, the more of your body is required upon it.

But we want our kids to learn far greater lessons that aren't part of formal academic curricula.

In bygone days, pains were taken to see that schoolchildren studied the biographies of great men of faith and valor, particularly those of the nation's founding fathers. They were encouraged to model virtues they found in these heroes. Patriotism flourished, prayers were said, and flags were respected.

Children pledged their allegiance to one great nation under God.

This simple phrase, considered a given when God was still acknowledged as the reason for that greatness, has recently come under fierce attack. The heroes of character who fought for the right of today's citizenry to attack it once pledged their lives, fortunes, and sacred honor to that battle. They never flinched when called upon to make good on those pledges. Today's unsung heroes do the same.

In his book *Faith of My Fathers: A Family Memoir,* Captain John S. McCain, USN (Ret), who spent five and a half years in the "Hanoi Hilton" during the Vietnam War and now represents Arizona in the United States Senate, describes the effects of an upbringing in faith and character:

> Every POW knew that the harder the war was fought the sooner we would go home. Long aware of the on-and-off peace negotiations in Paris, we were elated when the Nixon administration proved it was intent on forcing the negotiations to a conclusion that would restore our freedom. As the bombing campaign intensified, our

morale soared with every sortie. It was after one raid, and our raucous celebration of its effect, that the guards dragged Mike Christian from our room.

Mike was a Navy bombardier-navigator who had been shot down in 1967, about six months before I arrived. He had grown up near Selma, Alabama. His family was poor. He had not worn shoes until he was thirteen years old. Character was their wealth. They were good, righteous people, and they raised Mike to be hardworking and loyal. He was seventeen when he enlisted in the Navy. As a young sailor, he showed promise as a leader and impressed his superiors enough to be offered a commission.

What packages we were allowed to receive from our families often contained handkerchiefs, scarves, and other clothing items. For some time, Mike had been taking little scraps of red and white cloth, and with a needle he had fashioned from a piece of bamboo he laboriously sewed an American flag onto the inside of his blue prisoner's shirt. Every afternoon, before we ate our soup, we would hang Mike's flag on the wall of our cell and together recite the Pledge of Allegiance. No other event of the day had as much meaning to us.

The guards discovered Mike's flag one afternoon during a routine inspection and confiscated it. They returned that evening and took Mike outside. For our benefit as much as Mike's, they beat him severely, just outside our cell, puncturing his eardrum and breaking several of his ribs. When they had finished, they dragged him bleeding and nearly senseless back into our cell, and we helped him crawl to his place on the sleeping platform. After things quieted down, we all lay down to go to sleep. Before drifting off, I happened to look toward a corner of the room, where one of the four naked light bulbs that were always illuminated in our cell cast a dim light on Mike Christian. He had crawled there quietly when he thought the rest of us were sleeping. With his eyes nearly swollen shut from the beating, he had quietly picked up his needle and thread and begun sewing a new flag.

I witnessed many acts of heroism in prison, but none braver than that. As I watched him I felt a surge of pride at serving with him, and an equal measure of humility for lacking that extra ration of courage that distinguished Mike Christian from other men.[10]

From Freedom Fighters to Lotus Eaters

The essence of life comes to light in its simplest form for POWs. Existence is stripped bare of everything except what really matters. McCain recalls what inmates dubbed the "Church Riot" breaking out over the men's insistence to conduct services in their cell, reciting Scripture and singing hymns in defiance of their captors' orders. Three POWs were hauled out into the courtyard and marched off to the punishment cell the prisoners called "Heartbreak Hotel."

> As they were led out, Bud Day starting singing "The Star Spangled Banner," and soon every man in every cellblock joined in. When we finished the anthem, we started on a succession of patriotic tunes. The whole prison reverberated with our singing, and the wild applause that erupted at the end of every number. It was a glorious moment. Finally, the Vietnamese managed to disrupt our fun when they marched in en masse, arrayed in full riot gear, and broke up the party.[11]

McCain and his fellow prisoners held church every Sunday after that and by Christmas even prevailed upon their captors to bring them an English translation of the Bible, which they declared to be the only copy in Hanoi. "Hastily I leafed through its tattered pages until I found an account of the Nativity," McCain recalls. "I quickly copied the passage, and finished just moments before a guard arrived to retrieve the Bible. On Christmas night we held our simple, moving service. We began with the Lord's Prayer, after which a choir sang carols. Between each hymn, I read a portion of the story of Christ's birth from the pages I had copied. We gave prayers of thanks for the Christ child, for our families and homes, for our country."[12]

Now, these men were baby boomers, products of the '50s and '60s. Beyond a strong background in literature (McCain retold Kipling and Hemingway stories from memory for the POWs, as well as recounting classic movies), their parents had obviously raised them with a strong sense of faith in God and pride in their nation. Family, home, and country were in the fiber of their being, valued so much that they defied punishment to express them. Yes, prayer had already been abolished in the schools then, and texts had begun to be watered down, but accounts of the men who won our freedom still graced their pages, and the parental voice in education was much more honored than it is now.

Today children's perception of the founding fathers has definitely been reprogrammed, not to mention their perception of faith and family. A 1986 study of history textbooks found, after a perusal of all textbooks for grades one through four, "not a single reference to any contemporary American who was religious or engaged in any act of faith" and "no references at all to any child who prayed, went to church or temple." The same study found that textbooks for grades five and six went a step further, omitting all use of the words *marriage, wedding, husband,* and *wife.*[13]

"Proving that not even a Nobel Prize was proof against the editors of elementary textbooks," Sykes says, "one sixth-grade reader changed a story by Isaac Bashevis Singer to make it inoffensive. In Singer's original story, a boy not only prays 'to God,' but later says, 'Thank God.' In the educationist text, however, the editors removed the words 'to God,' and amended the phrase 'Thank God' to the apparently less offensive 'Thank Goodness.'"[14]

So God's kicked out, and the vacuum is filled with humanism today. People are wonderful. Children rule. Hey, we don't need to abide by God's rules anymore, kids. He's outdated. Who's in now is *you*. You're what it's all about. Who needs outside help, after all, when each individual is so wonderful, special, gifted, and uniquely talented? Forget about morals, values, duty, honor, and all that archaic stuff—especially learning—and let's just celebrate how wonderful you are. How can anybody doubt that you're tops, whether or not you've done anything of worth to substantiate that claim?

"Even a cursory knowledge of history would indicate that it is precisely that itch of self-doubt that provides the spur to human advance," Sykes says. "Take away the struggle, the doubts, and part of the chemistry of humanity is dissolved. A nation of explorers, discoverers, and freedom fighters becomes a nation of lotus-eaters and navel admirers."[15]

Let's face it: It's up to parents to bring kids back to reality and godliness in today's humanistic environment. So remember to teach all the things that aren't in the curriculum. Teach them to learn how to learn from the Giver of all knowledge, and they'll become lifelong learners, seeking the wisdom that really matters. Teach them that the world doesn't owe them a living; that whiners and winners don't mix; that they are called to excellence and to surpass the status quo and go far beyond average, because God will make them the head and not the tail (Deut. 28:13); that we must give the best we have, because we give it all as unto the Lord.

Then watch your children reap the blessings.

Train Up a Child

In equipping a child for life beyond the nest, two equations are vital:

> Love of reading + Excitement of discovery =
> Lifetime Education
>
> Love of God + Joy of living for him = Lifetime
> Blessings

The eagle builds her nest on the rocky ledge of a sheer cliff. She lines the nest with lots of soft down, but underneath the cushy layer, the bottom of the nest contains thorns and thistles and sharp rocks. This gal thinks ahead. She knows those ugly little eaglets with faces only she could love aren't going to stay ugly and soft and little. They'll develop mammoth wingspans and powerful pecs (without even pumping iron—how unfair is that?), and ultimately fly the coop.

But not without being given a strong hint.

When those soft little baby pinfeathers are replaced by serious flight feathers, the time has come to make the nest unbearable so that flying lessons can begin. That sharp stuff makes jumping out into thin air seem a desirable option. At first they must trust that Mom knows what she's doing. If they botch it, no sweat. She's still there to fly underneath and catch them. She only gives them over to solo flights after they've logged enough airtime to make her confident they're ready to wing it.

Then she launches them out there and pretends not to see how they tweaked their beaks on the first treetop they misjudged the height on. I dedicate this last comment to all you parents of teenagers. Some lessons are only learned the hard way. But the point is, they'll keep on learning as they grow, and they will become aerial acrobats in their own right. All the while, the blessings and destiny you spoke into their lives while they were still in the nest will cover those times when you have to wince and hand over the car keys.

Still, the moment we think we've arrived, someone moves the finish line. As Yogi Berra so memorably put it, "It ain't over till it's over." But the truth is, it's never really over. Because we haven't arrived. If we had, we'd already be basking in a hyperwhite cloud of glory in heaven's throne room. But as long as we're alive, we are in a state of flux. We must teach our kids to always be in discovery mode, ready to learn something new that they didn't know the day before, which will change them and cause them to grow as people.

Because when we quit growing and changing, we're dead.

By the same token, when we quit seeking God and growing on the vine (Jesus), we're spiritually dead. We'll dry up and blow away like an uprooted plant. Pinch a joint closed on a grapevine and in a day or two the whole branch withers away. Jesus said we have life only as we're abiding (living) in him. He's the vine; we're the branches. The moment you cut a branch off, it's next winter's firewood. Its source of life and strength is gone. We can only function in life if we stay connected to the vine.

Have we passed this life-giving truth on to our kids? Or have we left them in a vulnerable state in which they stand to gain the whole world and lose their own souls (Mark 8:36–38)?

Children must learn to have convictions. Where do you think they'll get them? Will they absorb them through their pores by osmosis? I don't think so. We live in a world that says there are no absolutes and that everyone makes up their own rules as they go.

Imagine if traffic flowed under such laws. In Mexico, for example, the law says that if you come to a four-way stop, whoever honks first has the right-of-way. Seems logical enough until you consider how hard it is to tell who honked first when all four arrive and honk at once. But each driver knows for sure that he honked first, so he can proceed. Must make for interesting traffic court debates.

Suppose there were no right or wrong side of the road. Many a tourist in England finds out quickly that the right isn't so right anymore. It only takes one heart-stopping incident to convince you the right side is wrong. There must be absolutes. You can't take a stand on both sides of the fence. Not with both feet, anyway. And not without serious consequences.

What, then, will cause your children to develop godly convictions? Do you think you can sit them down with a textbook and give them a course on values that will cause the root of godly conduct to spring forth and Christian virtues to blossom? Don't you wish it were that easy?

But God has a far better plan. It's called discipleship.

Welcome to the glass-house life. Part of your job description is transparency. Your kids are watching your every move, hearing your every reaction to life's situations and to the challenges brought your way for your growth. As you respond with godly convictions and talk about the Word of God as your basis for everything you do and say and decide, God honors that before your children. He blesses your life.

In turn, you pass blessings on to their lives. With or without words.

In Deuteronomy 6:6–9, God describes the discipleship process: Parents teach God's words to their children. When? When they sit in their house, walk on the road, lie down and rise up, binding them for continual signs upon their hands and between their eyes and posting them on the doorposts of their house and gates.

Hmmm . . . sounds like God's got the whole ball field pretty well sewn up. What does he expect? That you'll

129

keep your Bible duct-taped to your forehead and your kids duct-taped to your apron strings at all times so you can do all this teaching?

As a matter of fact, he does. In a manner of speaking.

There'll come a time when you cut those strings loose, stir up the nest, and push them out into the ionosphere to fly on their own. But in the meantime, God's Word must be "in your mouth and in your heart" (Rom. 10:8)—being conveyed to your children in action and word and attitude—morning, noon, and night. Your relationship with God must be a real, live, tangible thing that's so exciting to you that you can barely contain yourself for joy that it's yours if you expect it to be exciting to your disciples.

If it's not that exciting, then don't expect them to embrace it. They'll listen to the world and how excited they are about things that pass away. They'll wind up trying to straddle the fence, which only leads to disaster.

People riding the yellow line are generally playing chicken. Take it from Jim Hightower, former head of the Texas Department of Agriculture: "There's nothing in the middle of the road but yellow stripes and dead armadillos."[16]

Don't let your kids wind up as roadkill.

Lifesavers

1. God commanded Israel to be diligent in passing their faith on to their children and grandchildren by word of mouth throughout the day. Every day. Just think: They didn't have phones back then, or the Internet,

or Western Union. Not even the Pony Express! Still, the oral tradition handed down from generation to generation was the lasting and unshakable base upon which the entire Old Testament took shape.

And these words which I command you this day shall be in your heart. You shall teach them diligently to your children, and shall talk of them when you sit in your house, when you walk by the way, when you lie down, and when you rise up. You shall bind them as a sign on your hand, and they shall be as frontlets between your eyes. You shall write them on the doorposts of your house and on your gates.

Deuteronomy 6:6–9

2. Did they do it? How do you think nagging, finger-shaking Jewish mothers became so proverbial? Jewish fathers are pretty good at it too. For example, Jesse obviously taught his kids to give the tithe off the top of their day to the Lord, seeking him first thing in the morning and fostering a love for his Word, because his son, King David, said:

Give ear to my words, O LORD.
Consider my meditation.
Give heed to the voice of my cry,
My King and my God,
For to You I will pray.
My voice You shall hear in the morning, O LORD;
In the morning I will direct it to You,
And I will look up.

Psalm 5:1–3

We will not hide them from their children,
Telling to the generation to come the praises of the
    LORD,
And His strength and His wonderful works that He
    has done.

Psalm 78:4

131

3. Eunice and Lois, Timothy's mom and grandma, were God-fearing women who taught him the importance of the Word of God and labored in prayer to see God's gifting birthed into his life. Said the apostle Paul to his son in the faith:

When I call to remembrance the genuine faith that is in you, which dwelt first in your grandmother Lois and your mother Eunice, and I am persuaded is in you also. Therefore I remind you to stir up the gift of God which is in you through the laying on of my hands.

2 Timothy 1:5–6

And that from childhood you have known the Holy Scriptures, which are able to make you wise for salvation through the faith which is in Christ Jesus.

2 Timothy 3:15

4. Besides sharing their faith, these folks also passed on down-to-earth practical wisdom like the kind we spoke of earlier. Solomon told his son to get himself a job, to keep his nose clean and work hard before he could buy a house, and not to get into debt because the creditors would own him:

> Prepare your outside work,
> Make it fit for yourself in the field;
> And afterward build your house.

Proverbs 24:27

> The rich rules over the poor,
> And the borrower is servant to the lender.

Proverbs 22:7

A Function
of Dysfunction

Family Identity

One day, the father of a very wealthy family took his son on a trip to the country with the firm purpose of showing him how poor people could be. They spent a couple of days and nights on the farm of what would be considered an extremely poor family.

On their return trip, the father asked his son, "So what did you think?"

"That was great, Dad," his son replied.

"Did you see what I mean about how poor some people can really be?"

"Oh, yeah!"

"So tell me what you learned from this trip," his father prodded.

"Well, I saw that we have only one dog and they have four," his son said. "We have a pool that reaches out to the middle of the garden, but they have a creek that goes on and on forever. We have a few imported lanterns in the patio, but they have a million stars at night. Our veranda goes out to the front yard, but their meadows reach out to the endless horizon. We have a small piece of land to live on, but they have fields that go as far as the eye can see. We have servants who serve us, but they serve the needs of others. We buy our food at the store, but they get to grow theirs. We have walls around our property to protect us, but they have friends all around to protect them. Thanks, Dad, for showing me how poor we really are."[1]

Just as one man's trash is another's prized possession, one kid's less privileged family can be viewed by another kid as a fabulous adventure in growing up.

It's all a matter of perception, isn't it?

You can pick your friends, it's been said, but you're stuck with your relatives. Or, to put it more positively, you're part of your family for a reason. For good or ill, these people will have the most influence on your life. The good news is, as Christians, God's grace is upon our families, and since family dictates a large part of who we become as adults, growing up in a Christian family is a great blessing.

The better news: As home-based scholars, your children will learn to appreciate their family as a positive aspect of who they are. It's the first place they learn discipline and responsibility, love and trust, conflict and justice. In a homeschooling family, this education is ongoing, and as the child grows and changes within the arms of the loving family unit, he learns new things every day both about himself and others.

Part of a child's education is learning to appreciate his family as a gift from God. Too often we jump to the conclusion that we live in the most messed up family on the face of God's green earth. After all, we know ourselves. Worse, we know our siblings and parents. We live in constant fear that somebody will find out what a clueless bunch we really are.

My second son, Ben, sat in my brother Steve's Pennsylvania living room for seven hours while my older brother David bombarded us with forgotten anecdotes of our childhood years, some of which we'd never been aware of. The oldest of the three siblings, David has such a great memory of obscure events that I'm sure he could recount his birth in vivid detail. I, on the other hand, rarely remember what I ate for lunch an hour ago. Dave was facing a pretty tough crowd, as I didn't recall the tidbits he reveled in and they were mostly before Steve's time.

Many of these family gems were hard to believe. While I had to admit I didn't remember them, I surely wouldn't put them in the impossible category, given the nature of our forebears. We had some pretty colorful characters in our background. "We're only human" was an adage sure to have been coined by one of them, and it was undoubtedly an understatement in our family.

Ben had flown into New York from Ohio to be with me at my father's funeral. Though far from being an observant Jew (he'd consumed more than his share of shellfish, ham, and bacon), Dad had requested an orthodox Jewish service and burial, and the three of us had recited kaddish at his graveside. It had already been a weird weekend, and now Ben sat silent in the corner armchair, chin poised on hand, looking very much like Rodin's *Thinker* with a five-o'clock shadow. At length, David excused himself to return to New York, and Steve and I sat and tried our hardest to dredge up the memories he'd alluded to.

I turned to Ben.

"Are you in shock?" I asked. "You haven't said a word."

"Oh, no . . . just thinking."

"Are you enjoying our wild and wooly past? We weren't saved then, you know."

"Oh, yeah, I know. But that's okay," Ben said. "I always thought you guys were way too *Ozzie and Harriet* anyway."

Now, there's a reaction I wouldn't have expected from a kid who grew up in our own dysfunctional family. But the truth is, everybody's family is dysfunctional. Show me a "functional" family and I'll show you a high concentration of confined interacting neuroses on the verge of a collective mental breakdown.

But too often we focus so much on our families' familiar negative aspects that we forget what priceless treasures lie right under our noses, in our own homes, and instead we concentrate on what we perceive as the neighbor's better life on the other side of the fence.

Solomon said, "Where no oxen are, the crib is clean; but much increase comes by the strength of an ox" (Prov. 14:4). That's poetic language for "If you want to get the job done, you'd better be ready for some cleanup."

Remember, the grass is *really* greener where there's the most fertilizer.

In other poetry, the Bible says, "Pleasant words are like a honeycomb, sweetness to the soul and health to the bones" (Prov. 16:24). Those pleasant words aren't the first ones that spring to our lips in our moments of family friction. This is why we must offset the negative by building on the positive. Instead of wasting time bickering and picking at each other, try making a concerted effort whenever possible to speak uplifting words about your family that will show your kids how special God has made it and how privileged they are to be a part of it.

In our homeschool, we as a family are distinct from the next homeschooling family. Yet growing up learning how God has blessed the family and made everyone a

Family Ties

Homeschool: Where everything is relatives

The strength of your scholars lies in their family foundations. This is what gives them the edge, not only educationally but relationally, in matters of self-image and character building, faith and work ethic. Family impacts every area of who they become. You can give assignments that will help your kids appreciate where they've come from and where they're going. For example, they can visit great-grandparents and record an interview on their growing-up memories. Have them use it to make a report and construct a family tree. They can become pen-pals with distant cousins. They can interview siblings and write their biographies. Mom's and Dad's areas of expertise add flavor too. If you know a foreign language or play a musical instrument; if you are an expert typist, painter, or needlepoint artist; a cake decorator, architect, or interior design guru; a chef, cyclist, or birdwatcher, find enjoyable ways to incorporate these skills into projects with your kids. They'll learn who you are, create a link with you, and feel proud to be your protégé. At the same time you'll enjoy discovering who God created them to be. Learning new skills together is also exciting. Libraries, craft stores, and city parks departments offer many classes at reasonable rates that will thrill you both. Most of all, build your kids' family memories in stories, outings, vacations, church outreaches, and simple stories of times gone by recalled at the dinner table or family altar. Today's adventure is tomorrow's heritage.

special person within it can provide a child with pleasantly surprising revelations. These form a great part of his foundational concepts regarding his roots and how he's been divinely positioned to be who he is in God.

Something Told Me

Be sure to set aside time to tell the Story of You. The story of where your roots are sunk down on both sides of the family tree, the story of how you and your spouse grew up with your kids' grandmas and grandpas and your own, the story of how you two met and married, the story of how each of the kids was born, the story of the many places you've lived and the many pets you've had, the story of the multiple car breakdowns and plumbing disasters.

But most importantly, share the story of how each of you got saved and found Jesus and made him the Lord of your lives. Where would your kids be if you hadn't? These testimonies are foundational to your children's spiritual education, as are the ongoing testimonies that you'll experience as God showers you with his goodness during your lives together.

Family testimonies usually arise out of our most unlooked-for moments and in circumstances beyond our control. That's right where God loves them. When things look darkest, we learn to say, "Wow! What an awesome chance for God to show his power!" He must feel that way too, because he invariably shows up and does something wonderful. It's generally something designed to remind us that "it's not about us"; if it were we'd be sunk.

He's a pretty strategic thinker, God is.

One of our family's most enduring traditions is a Memorial Day camping trip to Turkey Creek in the Chiricahua Mountains. One such trip came at a particularly trying financial juncture. Three sleeping bags had decided they were overworked and underpaid, expiring into a heap of moth-eaten fibers. Camping equipment union rules clearly state that it's illegal for one sleeping bag to wear out at a time.

The neighbor's borrowed cargo trailer belonged to the same union. Waiting till we were crossing a cattle guard in the Middle of Nowhere (a specific location known to all seasoned campers), it developed a broken hitch, incapacitating our journey and requiring an immediate welding job. I wound up leaving camp the following day to visit the local emergency room with various and sundry female complaints.

By the time all ills had been cured, it seemed we would be arriving home considerably poorer—in fact, about two hundred dollars behind the budget. But while sitting by the side of the road near the cattle guard in the Middle of Nowhere, I mentally launched one of those not-so-formal prayer requests heavenward: "Hey, God, we're really gonna need some help here, you know?"

Fortunately, he didn't give me the same answer I give my kids: "Sorry, I'm not qualified to give the kind of help you require."

After five recreational days in the mountains, we were finally homeward bound, cruising down the interstate in all our glory. The car was full of kids who looked abundantly ready for hot water and indoor plumbing. The trailer was happy after its little fit and skipped along behind us, wearing a smile and a halo, carrying the spoils of war: flashlights with expired batteries, Coleman lanterns with disintegrated mantles, empty cooler chests, and dirty laundry.

We noticed a driver in the adjoining lane who kept matching our speed, beeping his horn, and waving to us. Bereft of brain cells, we waved back, thinking he was being friendly. After all, lots of people wave to big families on the road. They think they're cute, as long as they belong to someone else.

Finally the driver pulled ahead of us, slowed abruptly, stopped on the shoulder, and flagged us down. Chris pulled over. "Maybe there's something wrong with the

139

car," he said as he got out. After a short conversation, we saw the guy take off down the road.

Chris returned with two hundred dollars in his pocket. The guy had won a large amount of bingo money and said "something" told him to give us that exact amount. This time, it was a conscious prayer: "Thanks, God. We needed that!"

One of God's most often-used names is Something. But that's okay. He has a great sense of humor. Anyone who doubts that needs to spend more time looking in the mirror.

The mirror's a good place to discover who we are. But remember, it's not the image in which your kids have been made. And this is a good thing. When our daughter Naomi told us at the age of nine that she wanted to be a nurse, I knew she meant it and I had misgivings. I personally can't stand the sight of blood and deal with it only by the grace of God-given adrenaline in an emergency situation involving my own children. Even then, before I'd look at the actual wound, I'd lay hands on it (hard!—direct pressure and all that, you know) and pray, and ice it within an inch of its life, and run cold water over it till it turned blue. When it was bandaged, I'd go collapse somewhere, stare at the wall, and braid back together the frayed ends of my nerves.

I shared this with Naomi. She gave me a characteristically stubborn Maakestad answer: "But, Mama, that's you. And I'm not you."

Yes, well, thank God for that! It was a cute answer at nine and a mildly alarming one at fourteen. At seventeen she had completed all her prerequisites and was carrying a 3.75 GPA when she applied to the nursing programs at both Pima College and the University of Arizona and was politely told that after the interview process, she hadn't been selected. While you can't prove age discrimination in such a situation, you have to ask yourself why else she wouldn't have made the cut.

Because they didn't believe she could be serious at seventeen years old, that's why.

Not to be daunted, Naomi pulled money out of her own pocket and took a three-month CNA certification class, then took a job as a patient care technician at University Medical Center. After working there six months, she reapplied and was accepted by both schools, whose staffs now realized she was serious. Pursuing a bachelor's degree, she completed her RN program and worked another full year after graduation to complete several national emergency certifications so she could be an ER travel nurse. Now the travel agencies descend upon her with a fervor that makes sharks on a feeding frenzy look like vegetarians at a prime rib buffet.

Here's a girl who wouldn't take no for an answer because she knew what God had for her and wouldn't let anyone take it away. These are skills she learned from her dysfunctional homeschool family, where she first learned that it was okay to be ahead of the masses. To be confident in the calling God gives you and wait for the world to catch up with you and respect you. Or not. To practice reverse peer pressure.

Reverse Peer Pressure

Are you worried that home education is odd? Well, why be normal? Why conform to all the nonconformists who are all different the same way? It's like buying a "custom" home in a housing development. Now, there's a real misnomer. Sure, it looks like every other house in the neighborhood, but the garbage disposal's different, so it's unique.

Are you the only weirdo? Be proud and enjoy your God-given uniqueness. You're just ahead of your time;

the world's only now getting ready to get ready to accept home education. But who asked for their approval? Where would our graduates be right now if we had waited?

How did Moses stand up to Pharaoh and all of Egypt? Reverse peer pressure. How did Daniel, Shadrach, Meshach, and Abednego stand up to the king and all of Babylon? Reverse peer pressure. Okay, so he's the king. Big deal. So he's the Pharaoh. That doesn't make him right. And these people had the God-given guts to stand up and say so. Okay, there are the parts where they were banished from the kingdom and thrown into fiery furnaces and lions' dens . . . but, hey! Later they were promoted and revered!

Reverse peer pressure is another skill learned at home, a positioning imparted by family. Reverse peer pressure is a product of positive brainwashing. Princes and princesses are brainwashed from the time they are born to know that they have far greater responsibility and much more work to do because they are better and more special than the plebs. How much more special and better is a king's kid, a child of God?

There's one catch: You have to be willing to take the tomatoes to the face that come with sticking your head above the crowd. The natural reaction to such an onslaught is to bolt and run or duck down and fit in. In the army of God, neither is acceptable.

Josh McDowell said, "While we need to fear what our kids could be tempted to do, we need to be more concerned with what our kids are led to believe."[2] Beliefs are the foundation for ethics and actions. When your Christian kids leave the homeschool nest and go on to pursue a higher education, they'll likely face indoctrination by humanists who teach that no absolute truth exists.

Here's the right place to say, "Who said?" We must teach those kids while we have them at home that the Word of God is the ultimate authority, because it's certainly not a popular notion elsewhere. Their calling is to go forth into the world and question everything, not just roll over and accept it. *Oh, really? Who said? Was it the Committee of They? The Powers that Be? Who elected them? Why are they right?* It's okay to teach kids to challenge what they're taught, as long as you also teach them to be ready to back it up with the truth. Yes, teach them what the theory of evolution says, but also teach them how creationism disproves it. Require both. They'll need it later in life. They'll need it to be a witness for Jesus.

Naomi was studying premed courses on her way to her BSN when she encountered the biology professor she dubbed "Mr. Evolution." Here was a guy with a mission: to blast anything Christian, fundamentalist, and/or creationist. He had long despised Christian students because he had found they couldn't answer his objections on his scientific turf. When Naomi met his scoffing with scientific answers, he couldn't respond and found himself respecting her.

"I'm going to give you a book to read that will settle the matter," he finally told her.

"Fine," she said. "I'll trade you." She gave him a creation science book written by a geologist. They parted the best of friends, and he admitted she had raised doubts in his mind.

Naomi's also the first to tell us she's so glad her family isn't like everyone else's, and she's glad she was taught that it's okay to be wild and crazy. She's glad she grew up being told she may as well enjoy being weird and question why the rest of the world feels it's normal. Cutting-edge people are known to check out what everyone is doing and do the opposite. I guess that's what our family did, although it wasn't intentional. It was just the right thing to do.

We were always the weirdos. We did natural childbirth before dads were allowed in the delivery room and breast-fed when bottles were the rage and breast-feeding was disgusting, unsanitary, and degrading. We didn't feed our babies solid food until they had teeth. All the '70s experts said that two-month-olds must have cereal and fruit, so it could all go in one end and out the other without enhancing anything in between. At well-baby checkups, I was verbally bludgeoned for malnourishing my children. By baby number five, the trends had changed: Babies were no longer fed solids before six months of age. Just breast milk, vitamins, water, and juice. Suddenly we were commended for our progressive thinking.

We eventually survived the Dark Ages of homeschool and lived to see a better academic world dawn for parents. Now, in the Golden Age of the new millennium, we encourage our daughters to make use of everything available to them: Birthing rooms and the company of their husbands, friends, neighbors, and goldfish in the delivery room. The aura of the breast-feeding mom that's acceptable in today's society. And all the wonderful curriculum fairs and homeschool support groups.

Land Mines on the Road to Success

My brother Steve went through high school in seven years without repeating a grade. But I'll let him explain that phenomenon himself:

> That bit of trivia nearly cost me my first job interview. During my home high school years in the '60s and '70s, I did missionary work in Mexico, worked full-time, and got married. It's hard to keep the wheels of the educational machine humming when you don't have time to sneeze. The human resources department finally digested these facts and hired me on as a computer programmer.

Homeschool wasn't in the dictionary back then and hasn't made it into many today. Homeschool curricula didn't exist on the market in my parents' generation. But not to worry. Thanks to Mom putting her black-market phonics book to good use during the heyday of word recognition, I'm an anomaly in my own generation: an adult who can read, write, and spell.

Our vintage 1940s science textbooks had expected to comfortably live out their retirement on a Goodwill shelf. No such luck. My sister and I made fair use of them to produce our own rockets, insecticides, and gunpowder. And we never understood kids who had trouble with decimals. We learned our metrics from Mexican government textbooks and our Spanish from a college-level text.

Who knew this stuff was beyond the grade level of an eight-year-old? Guess they forgot to tell us that.[3]

My own high school education ground to a halt at age thirteen when Steve, my parents, and I left my birthplace in the Bronx for the Mexican mission field. Marriage, kids, and twenty-four years of homeschooling followed. While my youngest completed his high school diploma at home, I dove into the same correspondence school to get mine. Then I attended college classes alongside my poor kids. Actually, they admitted to enjoying it. Graduating with high honors and a journalism degree, this forty-six-year-old grandma addressed the class of 2000. About time!

In spite of the long journey, I learned something extremely valuable during all this: It's not about me, thank the living God. It's all about what he can pull off in spite of me.

God has positioned parents in the most strategic spot for maximum educational advantage with their kids, and he's gifted them with the most natural capacity to care about, nurture, and instruct those kids. But in the final analysis, homeschool takes up a lot of family time.

Our own perception of how that time is used makes it seem worthwhile or not.

We could chuck the kids out the door and have time to ourselves and then worry about the outcome for years and perhaps live to regret that decision. Sometimes we decide to jump in and homeschool and find ourselves regretting that too. We look at non-homeschool families and think how normal life would be if we hadn't made that commitment. We feel like the whole world's against us for a reason, and that we're just weird for the sake of weirdness, without making an impact.

We're the loving, concerned, ultrainvolved parents, and where does it really get us? Into a custom-fit straitjacket? Is it worth it? Do parental concern and involvement pay off? Are we making a difference or just knocking our heads against a wall? Are we putting in any mileage on the long road to success and recognition for homeschooling as a viable form of education?

It's taken a good thirty years, but, yes, inroads have been made. The Arizona Families for Home Education sent out a recent e-mail reminding homeschoolers to attend the National Homeschool Rally in Washington, D.C. Imagine! A whole national rally for homeschoolers! In the capital! Not just a support group, which I would have greeted with glad squeals of delight and tears of joy in the '70s. Not just a citywide or statewide meeting, which would have been a remote dream in those days.

A rally in Washington, D.C., giving national recognition to homeschool families!

Included in the program for this event was a free preview of a homeschool exhibit area in the capitol's west wing and the governor's proclamation designating the week of February 3 as Homeschool Week in Arizona.

It would have been inconceivable to us at the dawn of our homeschool career that such events would be a part of our future. It would have seemed even more improbable that a bunch of chickenhearted, unrefined, undignified, politically and socially incorrect parents could make such publicly acclaimed headway against a long-entrenched educational system.

God is certainly a big God.

But that same day, I got another e-mail. This one came from friends of ours who recently moved to California to pastor a church there. They passed along via cyberspace this alarming information about their new home state:

The Pacific Justice Institute proudly announces its first annual *Left Coast Hall of Shame Top 10 for the Year 2002:*

1. The 9th Circuit Court of Appeals ruled the Pledge of Allegiance unconstitutional because of the phrase "one nation under God."

2. The California State Superintendent of Public Instruction pronounced homeschooling illegal.

3. A new law was passed forcing abortion training for all gynecologists/obstetricians (AB 2194 - Jackson, D-Santa Barbara).

4. San Francisco judges were officially instructed not to participate or affiliate with the Boy Scouts.

5. Hayward Unified School District adopted a policy to allow teachers to "come out" in their classes and publicize their sexuality.

6. A union dues objector was forced to give dues money to Planned Parenthood, Gay and Lesbian Alliance, or the ACLU.

7. The Corona Public Library openly allowed young children to check out any R-rated movies they chose, without parental consent or notice.

8. While using a pro-Islamic textbook, students were required to enact actual practices of Islam, including adopting Islamic names, building model mosques, and memorizing scripture from the Koran.

9. The Elk Grove Unified School District required middle schoolers to hear a prohomosexual presentation

without prior notice to parents . . . just three months after they settled a lawsuit involving a similar violation of parental rights by their high school.

10. Hawaii police officers were told they could no longer say the words "so help me God" in their oath to serve.[4]

We must ask ourselves the hard questions: Is there anyone but parents who will care whether these things impact their kids? Is there any place but the home where these worldly influences can and must be combated?

Yes, inroads for homeschoolers have been made, but we must watch for land mines on our beachhead. We can't allow the world to infringe on the land we've taken for God in the hearts and lives of our kids and in our dysfunctional but blessed homes.

The battle we fight here in many ways resembles the Israelis' fight for freedom.

Despite the fact that the United Nations granted them a slice of real estate to call their own at the close of World War II, they continue to face real daily battles to keep that right. For every tree they've planted, every house they've built, every wedding and funeral they've attended, and every holiday they've observed, attendees have shown up with a tool in one hand and a gun in the other.

We're talking about the land God originally promised to Abraham in Genesis. These are his children and this is their inheritance, placed in their hands by their heavenly Father. But the right to keep their own turf is challenged daily. Because they're different. Because they're weird. Because they're dysfunctional. They're still fighting for the right to win back what God's already given them.

Just as homeschool families must continue to fight their own battles and win.

Lifesavers

1. God commands us to nurture our kids in the ways of the Lord. Here's the great part about that: The biblical parents who followed this command had the grace of God upon their lives and their families despite their imperfections. In fact, reading about the great fathers of the faith should be encouraging, because not a one of them came from a family without skeletons in the closet. The Bible is honest. It shows them all to be what our families are: dysfunctional but blessed.

And you, fathers, do not provoke your children to wrath, but bring them up in the training and admonition of the Lord.

Ephesians 6:4

2. Let's take a case in point: Abraham. He followed after God with his whole heart. Except for the little matter of lying about Sarah being his sister. He got punished for this misstep not once, but twice in the course of his wanderings. And still, God called him his friend. Why?

For I have known [Abraham], in order that he may command his children and household after him, that they keep the way of the LORD, to do righteousness and justice, that the LORD may bring to Abraham what He has spoken to him.

Genesis 18:19–20

3. No matter how weird, our families will be showered with the blessings of God as long as we're faithful and repentant like Abraham was. Was he perfect?

No. But he was repentant and totally in love with God. God promises grace upon such a man, as well as upon his family:

> The steps of a good man are ordered by the LORD,
> And He delights in his way.
> Though he fall, he shall not be utterly cast down;
> For the LORD upholds him with His hand.
> I have been young, and now am old;
> Yet I have not seen the righteous forsaken,
> Nor his descendants begging bread.
>
> Psalm 37:23–25

4. Somebody said that God gives us kids so we can grow up. I don't know if I'll ever grow up, but I do know a lot of stretching takes place as a parent. We definitely earn our Wheaties in the course of our parenting years and more so in the course of homeschooling. The Bible says the gray head is a crown of glory if it's found in the way of righteousness (Prov. 16:31). I'm glad it doesn't say in the way of perfection! But it also says that a gray head is crowned by grandkids. Hang in there and revel in your dysfunctional family with its dysfunctional parents producing dysfunctional kids. And when the battle's over, you can wear your crown:

> Children's children are the crown of old men,
> And the glory of children is their father.
>
> Proverbs 17:6

The House
You Have
with You Always

Getting Them to Quack in Unison

It's been said that children are a great comfort in your old age—and they can get you there faster too. It's a matter of public record that children and organization can rarely be mentioned in the same sentence. But Herbert Hoover said something equally true: "Children are our most valuable natural resource."

In the Word of God, the apostle Paul says to his disciples, "I will very gladly spend and be spent for your souls" (2 Cor. 12:15). How applicable is *that* to homeschooling! They can only be your little prodigies after they've been your little projects. But remember, your children are not just your students; they're your disciples. And they're worth every penny, every minute, and every prayer you'll ever spend on them to see that raw material get turned into a powerful finished product God can use.

The trick is to pull it all off without becoming a victim of Hurricane Homeschool. Or am I the only one whose house qualifies for federal aid from the disaster relief fund? In spite of my best efforts, my cobwebs have cobwebs and house multiple generations of cobs. My dust bunnies have dug themselves bunny holes and put up mailboxes. I don't go hunting in my fridge for leftovers either—they're more than happy to crawl out and meet me halfway. My teenagers should be so cooperative.

Ordering priorities is a big factor. It's not so much that you don't have time to give your child all that early input. You will use today's twenty-four hours for *something*. It's more likely that you've made the kids' lessons a lower priority in deference to something you've perceived as being far more crucial. The housework, for example.

Admit it, you obsessive-compulsive clean freak. You have to have a clean house or your blood simply stops pumping. Everything must be shrink-wrapped, sorted, labeled, and filed. You can't bear to sit down and do lessons unless the rain gutters are vacuumed, the bills are color-coded, and the best silver is polished. How messed up is that?

So this isn't about the time factor, is it? It's about the teacher's nervous twitch.

A simple solution to this dilemma lies within the short bodies of all that slave labor you gave birth to. This is the main reason they enacted all those child labor laws, and although they've succeeded in protecting our little angels from tyrannical bosses outside our homes, on the inside we still call the shots. Teens or toddlers, your kids should be your right-hand men and women. This is the only way you'll survive the house and be able to run a productive homeschool in it.

If you haven't done this already, consider it a mandate, not a suggestion: Run—don't walk—to the nearest quiet corner of your home. If no such corner exists in your home, I totally understand and deeply sympathize. In that case, the moment your poor, fatigued husband crosses the threshold and you give him a welcome home hug-kiss-dinner's-in-the-oven, have him stay and watch the little ankle biters while you speed off to the nearest fast-food joint, grab a coffee and a corner booth, and get down to business.

Arm yourself with pen and paper, and don't come up for air till you've scratched out a survival plan that will afford you two brain cells to call your own, rub together, and produce the vital spark that will power your home-school day. Here's how:

Write down each kid's name at the top of the paper and then think of all the wonderful chores they can do while you compile their lessons in the morning. Assign each child a room of the house to clean, dust, and vacuum. Assign dog feeding, cat feeding, bird feeding, and sibling feeding to the older ranks. Let the younger ones fold laundry—after a fashion.

Delegation is the key.

What does all this do for you? Tons! It gives you two seconds of your own in which to breathe a prayer and slap down lesson assignments on the table before they've finished their chores. If they squawk, just tell them work ethic is part of their curriculum.

Now, you have to be tough: Don't let that three-month-old give you that cute toothless grin and use her diaper dependency as an excuse not to wash the dishes.

And remember: The years when you most want floors that can be eaten off of are the ones when you can't expect them to be fit for it. But not to worry: They'll be eaten off of anyway. Because eight-month-olds have a superior talent for finding the yuckiest slime in the remotest corner regardless of how many times you cleaned today. So you may as well just make your decision: Settle for less house and more school. You'll have fewer migraines that way.

The Spongy Years

Putting your kids' education first is a difficult decision, given our obsessive-compulsive, overachiever nature as homeschoolers, but remember, you're the only one willing to be there for them in their earliest uncivilized years from birth through five.

The experts don't see this child till he's five or six years old, because they're not on the baby-feeding and mop-up brigade like you are. And all those years, your children are dying for intellectual input in their spongy receptive state. So who's teaching them then?

I'll tell you who. The real expert: Mom.

You've taught them everything they know about being a human during their most crucial and receptive years. They'll never learn so much so quickly again. On the contrary, they lose what little they did know at double the rate during their teenage years. Just trust me on this one.

But as you keep doing the mommy and daddy thing, you'll discover worlds of neat stuff about your small, developing disciples. Because it's precisely during these early, messy, uncivilized, politically and socially and anatomically incorrect years that your kids' quirks and tics show up and can be used to academic advantage by you, the observant and loving tutors.

You've logged a vast number of Pampers, pablum, and potty training miles and earned your badge as "educator of short people." Don't quit now at the turn of the tide because you feel overwhelmed. God's a God of order, and he'll help you bring organization out of the chaos.

Too many times we feel like throwing our hands up and saying we simply can't handle it. However, it's not

Cheap Help Is Easy to Find

But good help may be a little tougher to locate.

At two to three years old: Your children can bring you younger siblings' diaper change items and pick up toys.

At three to four years old: Can fold hankies and washcloths and dust lower shelves.

At four to five years old: Can fold larger items and put away own clothes, make bed, and feed pets.

At five to six years old: Can sweep floors, hang laundry or empty the dryer, dust most furniture.

At six to seven years old: Can vacuum and dust an assigned room in the house, and clear and set table.

At seven to eight years old: Can wash dishes or load dishwasher, mop floors, and dress younger sibling.

At eight to nine years old: Can feed and change babies, answer phone, clean bathrooms, and learn basic cooking.

At nine to ten years old: Can wash, dry, fold, and put away personal laundry; empty trash; and mind baby.

At ten to eleven years old: Can wash windows, do basic weeding, and do spring cleaning-type jobs.

At eleven to twelve years old: Can do heavier yard work, extensive cooking, and clean the whole house.

At twelve to thirteen years old: By now they're your built-in baby-sitters and pretty good tutors. Enjoy!

fair to God, after all the helpers he's given you, to accuse him of leaving you in the lurch. That's like the story of the lady who was stranded at home during a devastating flood.

As the storm pounded the valley, the floodwaters rose higher and covered her front porch. A man on a horse came by and offered her a ride. She said no, she was asking God to deliver her from the storm.

The waters inundated the bottom floor and she went upstairs and sat on the roof of the porch. A man came by in a rowboat when the water was at the eaves and told her to climb in. She gave him the same answer.

She had climbed to her last perch on the roof when a guy in a helicopter offered her a lift and she turned him down.

Then she cried out to God, "Where are you, Lord? I asked you to deliver me from the storm and nothing has happened." A small patch cleared in the clouds and a voice came back from heaven: "My daughter, I sent you a horse, a rowboat, and a helicopter. What more do you want?"

Don't blame God for your problems if you don't listen to his answers. He's there and is always faithful to send you all the help you need. But I doubt he would have struck Goliath dead on the spot if David had sat on a rock with his hands in his pockets praying, "Kill the giant, God. Amen."

Early Home Input versus the One-Eyed Monster

Most of us were born and raised in the TV generation. It's getting to the point where we need to help our kids redefine reality as what's *not* on the screen. Too often parents have been guilty of letting the one-eyed monster hold the child's attention while they're busy in pursuits perceived as more urgent.

If we subscribe to this practice, we toss away a chance to deposit something that will yield a hefty return. A chance handed to us alone, on a silver platter—the chance for early academic input.

Montessori-style early instruction is now at the root of many preschool facilities, where children are no longer just baby-sat but actively instructed. You'd be hard pressed to find a day care center that doesn't do something instructional during the child's stay with them. But the truth is that the kids these preschool instructors drool over the most are the ones whose instruction began years before—at birth.

Donna Cohn, supervisor of the Child Development Center at Pima Community College in Tucson, says:

> There are many teaching situations that occur in the home naturally, and a smart parent will seize the opportunity to instruct. You can have the child count cars, count red cars, count number of plates you're setting on the table, tell you the colors of the food, tell you how many strawberries are on the plate, and how many will be there if you add one more. An aware parent makes an ideal situation for learning out of everyday experiences. Most kids who have been home with Mom for the first three years of their life tend to show more social skills, such as sharing, and are better at speaking to adults. They come in knowing general basics like how to count. I have a little four-year-old girl who can say thirteen-letter words and know what they mean. She knows the names of the president and the governor and the mayor. You can tell she hasn't been ignored or stuck in front of the TV.[1]

Why wait until the child is having trouble at school because he was sat in front of the great baby-sitter, the TV, and treated like an end table for the first five years of his life? A proven pedagogical fact is that the more a parent holds, touches, sings, speaks, and reads to and generally interacts with a child from birth to five years

157

old (and beyond!), the more absorbent the spongy mind becomes.

In contrast consider this shocking scenario:

> Imagine a place that is designed to handcuff the physical environment, a monotonous place, with no great range of things to see or hear, with nothing very hard or soft, very loud or very subtle. Put infants on their backs in shallow cribs, make a rule that we never turn them over, rarely pick them up even to feed or change them, and give them the barest human contact. Attendants will not talk to them. This description refers to a real place, a foundling home in Tehran described by Wayne Dennis in *Journal of Genetic Psychology* (1960). Only 14 percent of the children were able to crawl *at the age of one to two years*. Only 42 percent of them could sit alone at this age and only 15 percent could walk alone *at the age of three to four years!*[2]

Bonding and Abounding

A foundational experience of a baby at home is the nurture and love of his parents. As he grows, he learns interaction, caring, respect, and teamwork, all of which are crucial to his development and learning in all areas of life, including academics and, ultimately, the workplace.

Carolyn Schlicher, a certified teacher, stays home and technically "home tutors" the five kids while her husband, Darryl, manages an applications/development team for a successful, privately owned company.

Carolyn has discovered that fringe benefits for women are built into homeschooling:

> What I've learned in the past six years of homeschooling multiple children is fairly simple: that women will be saved through childbearing (1 Tim. 2:15). But before

you think me a woman who wears only skirts and my hair in a bun, with no makeup (no, no, and yes, but only because no one can see me right now), let me tell you my now deeper understanding of that passage. Simply said: It's not about me anymore.

Sure, I love to hear about those women who find it a spiritual experience to knead bread with their daughters, and how others have graduated their children at sixteen, and how others have spent three months on a unit study dealing with the engineering principles of bridge building as they served as a family on a missions trip.

But that's not the epitome of homeschooling for me.

I love hearing the school-bus motor outside and then rolling over until the house wakes up. I have watched my children's jubilant play in the season's first snowfall while the neighborhood kids were sitting in a classroom somewhere. And I have taken vacations in March, just because I can.

Again, these are not icons of the homeschool experience for me.

I have dealt with skeptical extended family, raised eyebrows in the grocery checkout, people telling me I'm too liberal because I don't think homeschooling is required to be a godly Christian parent, and hearsay and television shows telling me I'm too conservative by representing homeschoolers as repressed, stubborn, miserable people. My daughter's tears over the phonics lesson and my son's crossed-arm pout over math are a battle, but they don't draw me away from what I'm convinced the Holy Spirit desires me to do.

Because it's not about me, after all, which is why that verse is in there. It's no secret we are selfish and pretty much need God to change us, and God, being the perfect God he is, knew that. He created us women with his own purposes in mind, and he knew we could cloak ourselves in good works—which tend to spring up from our hands fairly easily—and call it righteousness.

But he knew that it was only when we were at the end of ourselves, from the physical pain of labor and delivery or the emotional pain of immature children who can't yet understand the delicacies of relationships, that we would accept our desperate state and call to him to save us. And while my pat answer to those who ask why I homeschool is a simple and nonthreatening "Because it's right for our family," I know how deep the reasoning goes. Yes, I homeschool for academic reasons. Yes, I homeschool for godliness' sake. Yes, I rarely love it, but mostly like it and occasionally wish it away.

But I do it to save myself from myself via my children.

Because it's really not about me anymore, which is the best way to find out whom he has created me to be.[3]

Keith Geiger, in his 1994 *NEA Today* article "President's Viewpoint," says, "Home is where children best develop the attributes so crucial to learning—confidence, motivation, effort, responsibility, initiative, perseverance, caring, teamwork, common sense, and problem solving."[4]

But these subjects aren't taught academically. They're imparted on the hoof, deliberately, by supermoms. Supermoms like Carolyn who see how setting aside time to nurture reaps benefits for both kids and mothers. Consider the supermoms of the Bible. Jochebed not only hid Moses for three months in violation of the Pharaoh's edict, she trained Miriam to have enough common sense, faith, and guts to step in and speak to a princess on behalf of her baby brother. Mom was rewarded by being paid to nurse her own son and train him in the ways of the God of Abraham, Isaac, and Jacob for his five spongy years until the traditional weaning time arrived. Hollywood would have us believe that Moses just threw over his throne as an Egyptian prince one day and ran out on a wild impulse to suffer and die with the Israelites on the basis of a flashback, a dream, or an epiphany.

But Moses was human like you and me. Neither of us would do that. I don't believe Moses did either.

I believe a child's training from birth to five will determine the course of his later life. This is the real meaning of Proverbs 22:6. Train up a child when he's young—how young? The younger the better!—and when he's old he won't depart from it.

Hannah did such a great job of training up Samuel before delivering him to Eli (also at weaning, about age five) that he wound up replacing Eli and his degenerate sons as God's next judge and prophet of Israel.

Ruth was a supermom too. Here's a gal who wasn't afraid to be the only weirdo, because she knew that God was God. Not only did she kiss her sister-in-law and her pagan homeland good-bye in deference to the God of Israel but she passed that love of God on to her son, Obed. He passed it on to Jesse, who passed it on to his boy, King David, the man after God's own heart, Ruth's great-grandson and the father of Solomon, the wisest and richest king in history. And ultimately from the house of David came the Lion of Judah, the Messiah, Jesus Christ. Had she stayed in her comfort zone, Ruth would have totally missed out on her destiny in God. And so would her kids, and theirs.

Contact!

Are you feeling inspired now? Pumped up and ready to rumble? That's great! Hold that thought, because meanwhile, back on the planet right about now, you'll hear the distant shattering of glass and the inevitable summons: "Mommm!" Now, how is it again that a homeschool—as in a school in our home, with our kids in it—can ever be possible? Obviously, something's gotta give if you expect to run a homeschool in the midst of real life.

That something is a set of rules that will give you the upper organizational hand and bring order to the chaos.

The good news is that you can establish a brand-new set of homeschool rules that will set boundaries for behavior that weren't there before. What a great chance to lay down the law!

And you'd better lay it down. For your own sake as well as theirs, and for your own schedule as well as theirs. Not to mention your own sanity. Keep your ground rules carved in stone from day one.

The morning, for example, is sacred. Your mornings are the time when scheduling is most vital. Because if Mom's to function at all, she needs her mornings. But there's one catch: Only Mom can give Mom her morning.

I've been guilty of lying there in the early morning staring at the ceiling or checking the lining of my eyelids for cracks, and just listening to the stillness of the house. That blessed stillness that comes so rarely to the home of a large family like ours. Just listening to all the many wonders of nature—the dogs gleefully tearing each other apart in the crawl space under our mobile home, the first little birdies of spring chirping as they build nests in the fiberglass insulation behind the loose trim strip on the roof, the cat meowing around the lizard in her mouth for me to let her in with it.

I stretch. I sigh a contented sigh. I wiggle my toes and say, "Thank you, God."

And he answers, "Get up, you lazy bum! We have an appointment!"

He sure knows me, doesn't he? He knows I'd just lie there till noon if he didn't remind me this is the only quiet moment in my day to meet with him in his Word. Those wee-hour revelations are always the freshest, the most incisive—the only ones that can penetrate the gray matter that will be commandeered and melted down by short people sooner than you can say "sweet hour of prayer."

162

And that's precisely why, as soon as their eyelids fly open, your crew should know that they're to be busy about their morning responsibilities: business before pleasure.

Remember that wonderful list of morning chores you assigned for each of your offspring to do before breakfast? It should include such responsibilities as making their beds, picking up their rooms, dusting the living room, or folding clean laundry, and of course, reading their Bibles and praying. All of this keeps them gainfully employed so you can pull together brain cells, have time with God alone, and whip up an academic curriculum for each of them for the day.

That means that your assignment while they're staying busy is to career down the hall to the kitchen and grab your caffeine, chocolate, Captain Crunch, favorite instrumental CD—in short, whatever wakes up those dazed little brain cells enough for you to get before him and receive instruction, wisdom, direction, and peace that will see this school day through for you and your students.

This is the most important part of your day and theirs. Don't forget that you must have them pray and read their Bibles too. Trust me, you all need it. By the time they're ready, you're ready. You can eat breakfast half an hour before your scheduled start time for school and still have some moments left for cleanup. A clean kitchen also soothes the soul.

As for the troops, demand that chores be done on time or there will be no breakfast until they are completed. If lessons are scheduled to start before that happens, they'll have to wait for a recess and be hungry for a while. That's the nature of consequences.

Okay, yeah: I *am* Mrs. Tough Guy. But this is a mom desperation move in disguise. I've discovered that if I say, "Yeah, but" for every kid's excuse too often, the exceptions become the rule. If we keep pushing back lesson time for everybody, we'll wind up starting at noon, which can be a bit counterproductive. Let's put this into perspective: The first break is only an hour away, and your kids waited longer to eat when you were shopping together for their pet turtle in the mall for six hours last Saturday. They just didn't notice it as much.

When the clock strikes nine, you kick off your fourfold plan for success:

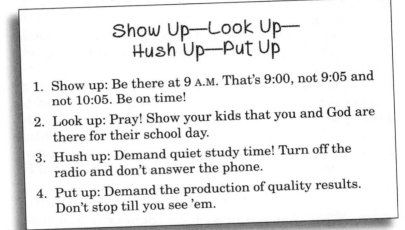

Show Up—Look Up— Hush Up—Put Up

1. Show up: Be there at 9 A.M. That's 9:00, not 9:05 and not 10:05. Be on time!
2. Look up: Pray! Show your kids that you and God are there for their school day.
3. Hush up: Demand quiet study time! Turn off the radio and don't answer the phone.
4. Put up: Demand the production of quality results. Don't stop till you see 'em.

That's right: Demand. Require. Pull rank. No questions asked. Never forget that homeschool is a contact sport. The rear must make contact with the chair. So don't go looking for the escape hatch on hairy days. Stick with it.

Life happens. Family invades. You get sick. The kids get sick. Or worse, your husband's home sick! Talk about *really* big monkey wrenches! On the hairiest days—if you can see them coming on the horizon—do a streamline job on the lessons. Just assign the most important stuff. Delay the composition and the science experiment and tack them onto a softer day when you don't care if they drop the match and burn the linoleum or a shorter sibling's hair.

Or double up the lessons and allow yourselves a day off—preferably one of those days that falls into the hairy category. But then you have to be ready for the heavy catch-up days. The days can ebb and flow.

Then there are the tidal waves, like when you've just given birth to a bouncing baby human. A whole week or two of lessons may get swallowed up in the great abyss. No sweat. Just wave a temporary white flag, go down with the ship, and resurface later. Tack those two weeks onto the end of the semester.

Face it: Homeschoolers are white-knuckle fanatics about everything in life. We're always harping on the kids, our husbands, and ourselves because we're not perfect. When we sit down and read a book for half an hour to breathe, we feel guilty. It's an occupational hazard of moms in general and of homeschoolers in particular. Relax! Get off your own back. Allow yourself to have off times when you're not firing on all cylinders.

Be human. But be a stubborn human. You and God can still do this thing together.

Smoke Signals

The sole survivor of a shipwreck was washed up on a small, uninhabited island. Being a religious man, he at once began to pray feverishly for God to rescue him, but as he scanned the horizon for help every day, none seemed forthcoming.

At last, mentally and emotionally exhausted, he determined to hunker down for the long haul. By and by, he managed to build a little hut out of driftwood to protect himself from the elements and provide shelter for his few possessions.

One day not long after this, he had been out scavenging for food as usual and returned to find his little hut in flames. As he watched the plumes of smoke rolling up to the sky, it hit him like a ton of bricks: The worst had happened. Everything was lost. Stunned with grief and anger, he fell to his knees and cried out, "God, how could you do this to me?!"

At a loss for how to proceed, he cried himself to sleep that night on the beach.

As the next day dawned, the man awoke to the sound of an approaching ship. He watched in open-mouthed amazement as a boat was lowered and three men rowed up to the beach.

"We're here to rescue you," the captain said.

"But . . . how did you know I was here?" the man asked.

"Well, of course, because we saw your smoke signal!" said the sailors.

Sometimes it seems as if everybody and everything is against you and you'll never get the kids through this grade in the next fifteen years, and nothing in your life will ever be clean and presentable again, and you'll never have a split second of time to call your own, let alone read that stack of books that's piling up on the night table.

Okay, so maybe I just described *most* of your days.

We haven't even considered the days when your time is called upon for bill paying and telephone answering and carpooling and potty training and counseling and boo-boo kissing and hair cutting. And that's just my short list.

Next time you feel like everything's just caving in—like your little hut is burning down to the ground—remember: It may just be the Holy Spirit sending up a smoke signal to summon the grace of God to come to your rescue.

How could we ever hope to homeschool without his grace?

Read the Fine Print

In order to communicate homeschool excitement to your kids, you must maintain your own enthusiasm within. Now, we've all had days that lacked in homeschool enthusiasm. That's because of another occupational hazard: We're human.

In Mom's case, make that two occupational hazards: She's also female.

So occasionally, we must psyche ourselves up and regain that enthusiasm.

Next time you're flopped on the bed with the door closed, trying to grab your kids' lunch break to destress, remember that there are teacher perks.

Not the least of these is the companionship of your children. Sometimes you don't feel very companionable and they're the last ones you want to "companionize." But let me tell you from the other side of the homeschool experience: One of the best things we've gained as a family is a closeness and friendship that extends way past their school years, into marriage and beyond.

My girls are all twenty-plus now, and two are moms. Every so often we'll get together for a girls' day out, ditching the kids with the daddies and taking a few hours to carouse and enjoy each other. Recently we ganged up on Debbie's nursery and redid it in Suzy's Zoo creatures and crazy little bulgy-eyed bugs wearing tennis shoes. We painted a lavender sky with white clouds and a big yellow sun with a smiley face on the top half of the room. The bottom half got the down-to-earth treatment with loads of tulips and grass to house the bugs. Deb painted Suzy herself peeking out from behind a tall clump of grass.

It looked great, but we needed a wall border to divide earth from sky at the horizon. We descended upon the nearest Home Depot and thumbed through several cata-

167

logs till we found the perfect design. By that time, we were in high gear from laughing at patterns and at each other. As the check-out guy rang things up, we jammed à la *Saturday Night Fever* to the rap music pulsing from his countertop boom box.

"Okay, you guys are having way too much fun," he said.

You can't beat that for a great opening to tell him it would never be this way but for the grace of God in our lives. I'd rather have these guys want what we've got than see 'em cringe in fear that we might be contagious. It's hard to be a witness for the joy of Jesus if you walk around baptized in cider vinegar. That nonsensical fun and closeness was built by God's grace while the girls grew up.

And, looking back, I'd say without hesitation that some of the best years of God's most awesome grace in our lives were those we spent together in homeschool.

Lifesavers

1. Solomon was a wise guy. A really wise guy. The wisest of all guys, in fact, because God granted his request for wisdom, as recorded in 1 Kings 3:7–14. And he used his gift of wisdom, well . . . wisely. He used it to pass on great knowledge and instruction to his son in Proverbs and Ecclesiastes. And from his writings, Solomon obviously feared God. And homeschooled his kids with his wife.

   The fear of the Lord is the beginning of knowledge,
   But fools despise wisdom and instruction.

My son, hear the instruction of your father,
And do not forsake the law of your mother;
For they will be a graceful ornament on your head,
And chains about your neck.

Proverbs 1:7–9

2. King Solomon also knew the awesome value of a
parent making early deposits in a child's life:

Train up a child in the way he should go,
And when he is old he will not depart from it.

Proverbs 22:6

Cast your bread upon the waters,
For you will find it after many days.

Ecclesiastes 11:1

and the value of a parent's godly example:

The righteous man walks in his integrity;
His children are blessed after him.

Proverbs 20:7

3. He also remembered to teach his children the most
valuable of all lessons—to seek the Lord while they
were young and not waste their early years when they
could be living for him and reaping the benefits:

Remember now your Creator in the days of your
youth,
Before the difficult days come,
And the years draw near when you say,
"I have no pleasure in them."

Ecclesiastes 12:1

4. You must be your children's first example of godliness
and the fear of the Lord. Teach your kids that wisdom

169

and academic education must go hand in hand if they
are to see the blessing of God upon their future:

I will behave wisely in a perfect way.
Oh, when will You come to me?
I will walk within my house with a perfect heart.
I will set nothing wicked before my eyes;
I hate the work of those who fall away;
It shall not cling to me.
A perverse heart shall depart from me;
I will not know wickedness.

Psalm 101:2–4

My son, keep my words,
And treasure my commands within you.
Keep my commands and live,
And my law as the apple of your eye.
Bind them on your fingers;
Write them on the tablet of your heart.
Say to wisdom, "You are my sister,"
And call understanding your nearest kin.

Proverbs 7:1–4

5. God puts great premium upon parents investing their
   hearts and lives into seeing their children become
   something special in him. If you're putting this task
   on the back burner, you've got it all wrong. Pull it up
   front and stoke the fire, because everything depends
   on it. Literally.

And he [Elijah] will turn
The hearts of the fathers to the children,
And the hearts of the children to their fathers,
Lest I come and strike the earth with a curse.

Malachi 4:6

Not only that, but your children/disciples will be
your greatest reward:

170

For what is our hope, or joy, or crown of rejoicing? Is it not even you in the presence of our Lord Jesus Christ at His coming? For you are our glory and joy.

1 Thessalonians 2:19–20

The Agony
and the Ecstasy

Ground School

"I could never teach my kids at home, because they won't listen to me."

When parents have laid faulty ground rules for a basic disciplinary relationship in their home, the word *home-school* can cause them to tremble.

How can I possibly teach my kids? What if they won't listen? What if they won't do their work? What if they talk back to me? What if they won't sit still?

Take heart. You're about to boldly go where you have never gone before. Exploring uncharted worlds gives you a great chance to rewrite the prime directive and establish a new set of disciplinary "school rules" that will give you the upper hand in other areas of life as well.

Novelty and high adventure are on your side as you begin to homeschool. We're all a bit schizophrenic, you know. In this case, that's a really good thing. Just call in your alter ego as backup. A mild-mannered parent need only change hats in the nearest phone booth to emerge as Supermom the Disciplinary Teacher, a highly respectable entity that didn't exist a moment ago.

You can wear the white hat and the black hat; be the good guy and the bad guy; separate the teacher persona from the parent persona, the strict no-nonsense-toe-the-line persona from the mushy-hugs-and-kisses persona. In the midst of a Klingon uprising, Supermom's at the transporter controls. Just utter a simple sentence like "We're in school now; that'll have to wait," and watch those little critters get beamed into instantaneous obedience.

Perhaps there's been a problem because you've been using the whoop-and-holler approach—where you whoop the kid's backside and holler at him. You know, the method that never works because he's built up an immunity to the same old response. Or maybe you do the whoop-*or*-holler—just holler at him and let him ignore you because you and he both know you never do any whooping. Either way, he wins and you lose.

Try instead the following equation: Discipline = Correction + Affection.

Don't raise your voice. Don't lose control. Don't rant and rave. Simply impose consequences. Then add a dash of affection when the lesson has been learned. This method proves so much more effective.

Suppose, for example, that your prodigy has spent half the morning alternately staring into outer space through the dining room wall, picking her nose, and dissecting her eraser. Her spelling words—the first lesson of the day—still lay ignored and unstudied on the table, and it's already 10 A.M. What should you do? Casually mention that anybody who finishes her lessons by lunchtime

173

gets to have a picnic in the backyard—and that if *all* students finish by lunchtime we get to go have a picnic at the park and play on the playground toys. Now go about your business and wait for results.

When the clock strikes noon, don't back down or shift gears. Make it stick. If your student has picked up the pace and finished, she's rewarded with a picnic, high praise, hugs, and kudos. If not, she watches her siblings get rewarded with a picnic out back, high praise, hugs, and kudos; and you tell her she's missed out. If all the other siblings have finished and are geared for the park but she hasn't, give hugs and kudos and tell them sis didn't quite finish but she'll do better next time. Sorry. Give her a hug too and tell her you're sorry it has to be this way and you know she'll do better tomorrow. I promise you: She will.

Peace in the Valley

Things will never be perfect, that's for sure. But I thank God that in the midst of the pandemonium of a homeschool household, he's always at work if we allow him to be. Jesus said, "My peace I give to you; not as the world gives do I give to you. Let not your heart be troubled, neither let it be afraid" (John 14:27). He knows us, doesn't he? He knows we'll occasionally freak out trying to do this thing and go off looking to find that peace on our own.

You can try meditation, yoga, and mind tricks, and maybe you'll fool yourself into some sort of temporary relief. You can run down the hall to the bathroom cabinet and pop a passel of ibuprofen or Tylenol and get relief that way too. But why settle for the temporary stuff when you know you need it all the time? Would you contemplate years upon years of a homeschool career without God's help? Not an exciting prospect.

An underlying current of ultimate calm lives in the spirit of the child of God, giving you the power to take on the world. It's what keeps you from having a nervous breakdown when nothing goes right for an entire semester, and all your relatives are harping on you and telling you your child is going to be educationally deficient, and the sewer backs up at the precise moment that your in-laws ring the doorbell for a dinner invitation.

God's peace is the superglue that holds the frayed ends together when you're at the end of your rope. When you let the peace of God reign in your heart and your home, he'll make you appear graceful and serene, like a beautiful swan. Sure, she's gliding on the surface, but underneath she's paddling like mad! But paddling is okay. Paddling isn't a lack of faith. But when we start believing all that paddling is actually powering the motor, we run aground.

As the moms, part of our job description is keeping on top of things and running the house and the school as administrator, but not as the main cheese. If I hadn't had the genuine peace that only Jesus can give me—the peace that the Bible says passes all understanding—every single day that I homeschooled, day in and day out, week in and week out, over a period of twenty-four years, I know for a fact I would have thrown in the towel, thrown up my hands, and shrieked, "No way! There's absolutely no way I can do this!"

And I would have been absolutely right. Nobody can do it without power from on high.

If you're at your wit's end and don't know how you'll ever pull this thing together, let me tell you: You aren't going to do it without letting go and letting God. If you haven't yet, ask him into your heart as the Lord of your life (a.k.a., Caller of the Shots). Admit you've given it the good college try and messed it up royally. That you're just a sinner like everybody else (Rom. 3:23) and that you need forgiveness and help (Rom. 6:23). Step down from the throne of your heart and give it to him as his rightful place. Step back and let him have his turn (Rom. 10:9). Permanently. Then, as his peace floods your heart, you'll find the stabilizing undercurrent that makes you able to face anything—even homeschooling.

Maybe you've already known that peace but you've forgotten to rely on it.

One of my favorite verses is Psalm 55:22: "Cast your burden on the LORD, and He shall sustain you; He shall never permit the righteous to be moved." The Message version says, "Pile your troubles on GOD's shoulders—he'll carry your load, he'll help you out. He'll never let good people topple into ruin." I like this rendition because piling my troubles on God's shoulders brings to mind the image of lifting great big bags of weight and worry off my own puny shoulders and transferring them to God's great big, broad ones—where they should have been in the first place! Now that's how I spell relief!

Some days I consciously pray it as a prayer: "God, I'm not going to let everything get me down. I give you these burdens. By an act of my will, I take my hands off them and I pile them on you." And he's so nice, he's always there to take them from me, again and again. It sure takes a load off my mind that shouldn't have been there in the first place. What was I thinking?

Are you trying to handle everything yourself? Just remember one thing: Everything belongs to God, not to you. If you'll just hand over the baton and give up your post as conductor, he's got your whole symphony orchestrated. Yes, you and God can do this thing. Just step down from the podium and let the music play.

Remember that peace that only he can give needs to reign in our homes before it can reign in our homeschools. Otherwise we're so uptight being the disciplinary teacher we forget to be the loving mom. Yes, our two roles need to be separated, but they must still both be present. Ask God to help you love those kids with his love and see them as he does. You'll be surprised at the tenderness and wisdom that will come to them through your mouth and through your heart as God takes over the reins and loves them through you.

And nobody could love them more. Not even you!

Tough Love

God is love, the Bible says (1 John 4:8). It also describes our God as a consuming fire (Heb. 12:29). How can these two attributes be reconciled? Easy: God is a holy God. He can't condone sin, so he made a way for us to escape our sinful nature so that he could have fellowship with his children whom he loves.

Correction and affection go hand in hand. Transgressions must be corrected. Affection must always be present, even in the background of correction.

But rules must also be rules. They must be enforced and backed up. So be sure that your ground rules include basic guidelines like these: No answering back to the teacher. The teacher knows better than you. That's why she's the teacher. No saying, "This is too hard." Of course it's hard; that's because you haven't learned it yet. When you learn it, then it'll be easy.

Surprisingly, commonsense answers like these are accepted without question, as well they should be. But you must take a stand and give the answers when things are challenged.

Answer objections with reinforcement and with God's Word. Never accept "I can't" from a student. Philippians 4:13 says they can do all things through Christ. This should be one of your first assigned memory verses. "I can't," when read between the lines, also means they don't

177

think they're smart enough. That means that somehow, somewhere, God messed up. This is unacceptable. Tell them, "Of course you can, because God made you smart and because he's going to help you if you ask him to."

"I don't want to" is one response that never ceases to amaze me. "So who asked you?" is what comes most quickly to my New York lips. But don't throw away the golden opportunity to challenge this kind of reasoning and point out that in the real world, nobody really cares what you want. Go ahead and hammer it home: "So who said anything about wanting to? Did I ask you if you want to? No. Do you think Daddy goes to work because he wants to? No. Then why do you think he goes to work? You know why? Because it's his job. School is your job. Some things in life you just do because you have to, not because you want to. That's part of being big and grown up and responsible, like Daddy. You can only be in school because you're big enough. You're not a baby. Babies just sit around saying 'I want' and 'I don't want' all day long, because that's all a baby knows. Your baby sister isn't big and grown up like you are, so she doesn't get to go to school. But when she's big enough, we'll let her learn important things just like you."

In short, don't coddle. Don't wimp out. Rise to the occasion and demand excellence. Go ahead: Require more of your kids than you think they're ready for. They've probably been ready for several months. Kids are experts at pulling the wool over adult eyes. They're also great at avoiding work. By the time they're teenagers, they've elevated it to an art form.

Demand a lot, and when you get it, be sure it's rewarded. But only reward truly good work. If mediocrity is rewarded, the reward loses its meaning. The same goes for grading. You can't just go around slapping *A*'s and smiley faces and scratch-and-sniff stickers and gold stars on everything, or they won't mean excellence anymore. They'll mean good ol' Mom thinks everything her kids do is great 'cause they're her kids and they're so wonderful. So why should they even try?

No, no. Make them earn it. Bye-bye, mushy Mom. Hello, Superteacher.

Incidentally, you don't just grade any old paper that crosses your desk. Only grade the worthy candidates. Too many wrong answers should indicate to you that there's been no absorption of knowledge. Don't just give it a lower grade. Send it back on a stretcher bleeding red ink and have it redone correctly. If they stop reading and cut right to the study questions, it becomes pretty obvious. In that case, have them read the material to you out loud—loud enough for you to hear from the next room as you go about your business, because I hope you know you're not going to be chained to the desk while they dawdle around with what they should have done right the first time.

Reinforce, yes. Encourage, yes. But at the same time, don't budge an inch.

I know what you're thinking: *They're already doing the best they can.* That just means they've already got you conditioned to accept substandard work. Don't settle for mediocre. Ask for more. Demand the best. Challenge them to higher levels, then stand back and let them amaze you. Untapped veins of gold are waiting to be mined in there.

The Bible says that whatever we do we should do heartily as unto the Lord. That translates into homeschool jargon as follows:

"Would you turn this paper in to Jesus?"

"Mommm . . ."

"You're saying you would? With this ketchup on it, and the yucky dirt smears?"

"No . . ."

"With this sloppy writing? With these misspelled words that you just studied last week?"

"But it's a whole 'nother week later. I can't remember 'em that long."

"You can do all things through Christ who strengthens you."

"Mommm . . ."

"You can even remember spelling words! Now, I know you wouldn't turn this paper in to Jesus. And that means you're not doing your best as unto the Lord. So here's a clean paper; go try again. I know you can do a great job. Show me how beautiful you can make it, and I'll give you a prize."

The Carrot versus the Stick

Bribery? You bet!

How excited would you get if your boss told you that paychecks for this week have been abolished due to lack of interest on the part of the management? Why do credit card companies offer introductory interest rates? Why do apartment complexes advertise a free month of rent? What if there was no toy in the Happy Meal?

Adam and Eve proved for all time that human beings are born with those immortal words "What's in it for me?" on the tips of their tongues, with "Why should I?" and "Who says?" running a close second and third. All work and no play makes Johnny certain that homeschool's a drag. It's not worth it to you or to them to keep their noses to the grindstone so long that it singes the eyebrows. Lighten up. Have fun.

If you expect to see some decent output, you need to be fair to your kids. Reward their efforts. Human beings don't function well without being given a vision for future rewards. There must be light at the end of the tunnel. That's what we call motivation. And motivational speakers agree that you can only get a donkey to move in one of two ways: with a stick on the rump or a carrot at the nose.

Most often, the carrot works better.

Now, we're not saying our kids are donkeys, although they do have their stubborn moments. Don't be discouraged. Kids aren't that hard to please. Just knowing that you love them and want to spend time with them doing something relaxing that doesn't resemble school can be a great reward. But I have to tell you: That simple picnic in the backyard was one of our bigger prizes. Amazing amounts of output were achieved with much smaller bait.

"You know, Mom, I can't believe how much work we used to do just for one little Brach's candy," my oldest told me recently.

"Whaddaya mean, one little Brach's? You guys got three!"

"Ohhhh, no, we didn't! It was three only if we finished by the first break. It was two for finishing by lunch and just one for finishing our lessons for the whole day at the regular time."

"So you want a brass band? Public school kids don't get anything for finishing."

"Oh, hey, I'm not saying it was a problem. What do you think *my* kids are getting?"

I guess the Brach's company will be around for a while, as long as we keep all those homeschoolers in prizes. But we had something bigger than Brach's, bigger than picnics, bigger than trips to the library and fifty-cent ice cream cones on the way home, bigger even than meeting Dad in the park for an evening barbecue and swim! The biggest prize of all was anticipated for months, because it came just once a year: the annual Maakestad school show.

Eyes on the Prize

We all need our just deserts . . . and other goodies.

Candies, trail mix, fruit, cookies, cheese, fruit roll, or other small treat

Certificate of honorable mention posted in conspicuous place

Privilege of reading a special book, playing a game, or watching a video

Picnic lunch in the backyard and a game of Frisbee, horseshoes, etc.

Water balloon fight or snowball fight, depending on season and location

Running in the sprinklers or sledding, depending on season and location

Afternoon picnic in the park and trip to the library

Chance to accompany Mom on a special errand or outing

Meeting Dad at the park for BBQ dinner and evening swim

Choice of special dessert for dinner

Choice of special afternoon outing

Privilege of accompanying Dad to work or a special outing

An earned day off from school for scholars who have worked overtime

Just remind the kid that if this paper is gorgeous, he'll get to hang it up for Dad and all the grandparents to see; that if he does a killer report, he'll get to read it for them; that if he practices this piece till it shines, he'll get to play it for them, and watch those students raise the bar all by themselves.

School shows leave report cards in the dust. This is no dispassionate listing of cold black-and-white letter grades grudgingly awarded for an entire semester of effort. This is a loud, wild, school's-out-for-the-term party, complete with crepe paper, balloons, and confetti; a special meal and a decorated cake; and stage curtains, full soundtracks, and special effects. Each scholar's best work is plastered all over the walls to be admired; award-winning compositions are presented by the awardees; Bible passages, poetry, and factual memorizations are recited; musical recitals and demonstrations of skill are presented to thunderous applause; and grade school and high school diplomas are awarded with appropriate pomp and circumstance.

And just so it doesn't get too dull and boring, the students are permitted the last word: a theatrical presentation cooked up on their own for the sole purpose of entertaining the audience. This usually takes the form of a puppet show, a magic show, a fractured fairy tale, a fractured Bible story, acrobatics, juggling, or whatever nonsense the participants deem appropriate.

Now lest you think this was all play and no work, we must hear the flip side from Dina, my oldest:

One of the basic responsibilities of the oldest is to be the great organizer. I found it my job to produce the school show in which we recited things we'd learned during the year, with a few extra memorized books thrown in for effect. We committed a month's worth of stuff to memory in the space of a week and put on a full stage production complete with lights, props, and key grips. The productions grew lengthier every year, but I suppose the extended family, dragged out to witness this blessed event, was impressed, since they kept coming back.

I eagerly anticipated the day when I'd graduate and abdicate my post as school show directress. But Mom—whether due to her Jewish upbringing or life in New York, or Lord only knows what else—was not one to allow family traditions to lapse so easily. Even while attending college, the unwritten law required me to remain at my post. In fact, for the first two years after I was married, Mom called to ask if I would please come over and organize my brothers and sisters and help them get this thing together because it just wasn't happening.

Yep, those poor firstborn kids. We rejoice in them and lean on them and spend the rest of our adult lives apologizing to them. Somehow she survived though. Just last year we attended the first annual Gastelum school show and watched her kids perpetuate this family tradition. After all that hard work all year long, we felt we should rejoice with these kids and give them at least part of the recognition they'd earned. A party still seems most appropriate.

And after the confetti is swept away, the ultimate reward arrives: summer vacation.

It makes facing another long school year bearable. And it's good for the kids too.

Tough but Human

That's right: summer vacation. Those two words go together like white on rice. Now, step in and test-drive these two babies: weekends off. Yep, those two words were made for each other too! Just stand in front of the mirror and repeat them five times each. Make sure you enunciate slowly and emphatically. Good. Now go to the blackboard and write them a hundred times.

That's no—as in *n-o, no*—absolutely *no* weekend or summer lessons!

And no, you may not take schoolbooks on the family road trip to make up for lost time! Talk about cruel and unusual punishment! These are kids, remember? *Your* kids! Not just your students. Let them be kids! Free summers and weekends are essential kid ingredients.

Time off for your kids is a must! Think about it: When will their gray matter recuperate? When will they remember they're not forty, gray, and paunchy? When will they get to pull the cat's ears and decorate the bathroom mirror with toothpaste and hide their dirty socks under the couch cushions and their gum inside the dictionary?

How can you make them sit at the table doing schoolwork while they watch the public school kids frolic past their window, playing and cutting up and enjoying life where the sun is shining and the birds are singing and all is right with the after-school world?

Open the door and give them a passport to nonacademic freedom. Let them have a social life. Knowing how to interact with people as well as with textbooks is a definite positive step toward a well-adjusted adult life. And as a well-adjusted adult, you need to interact with them.

Be sure you disengage superteacher mode during these times. Just cut up and be Mom who's not perfect. Let them cut up and be kids who aren't perfect. That means you're allowing them the luxury, because you already know they're not and you're cool with that.

How perfect they *aren't* shows up glaringly well in the way they clean (or not!) their rooms or do the chores they're assigned. Does this mean you should spend your life picking up after them and redoing everything? Not if they're going to learn. Guess what? You're learning too. You're learning patience and forbearance. Isn't God good?

But it does mean settling for less than perfection until you can demand more. Cut those kids some slack. Let them make a few mistakes. At least till they're three, don't expect the job you gave them to be done as well as you'd have done it. A good rule of thumb is "Hey, it's better than nothing . . . kind of." So they're not perfect yet. That's a good thing. After all, they have to live with *you!*

Now, wait a minute. Didn't we just say we should demand excellence from our kids? Well, yes, but that's on a *kid* scale of one to ten. They're kids, okay? Not short adults.

So ask yourself: Is this excellent output for their age and ability? Well, then, it's excellence.

Yes, demand a lot—but don't be a nonstop, implacable, obsessive-compulsive, ultra type $A+$ homeschool teacher. In other words, step out of character for a moment. Console yourself in the knowledge that it'll get better someday.

When our boys were teenagers, they could make rocket engines from paper-towel tubes and assemble entire computer systems from chips, screws, and wires. They tore apart and rebuilt cars from the ground up. One of our guys now works as a cutting-edge design engineer for an auto manufacturer.

Impressed? Please—don't be. No, really, don't. These same rocket scientists, computer geniuses, and design engineers couldn't figure out how to install a new toilet paper roll on the bathroom toilet paper holder. But, hey, neither can my husband, the computer-aided drafting specialist who leaps tall buildings in a single click of the mouse.

Sell Your Customer on the Benefits

What makes you excited about a product? Is it because the manufacturer's guarantee runs out the day after the product is designed to break down? I don't think so. You only buy the face cream because the model has no wrinkles, and the diet drink because the babe on the can has never had an overweight day in her life. And for just one half a moment, while you're slapping your money down on the counter, you really believe you're going to look like that. It's one of the downsides of being human: self-deception.

But consider how much easier it is to sell a product when all the claims about it are true. Such is the product you have to offer your offspring. Homeschool really is loaded with benefits, if you're keeping those benefits intact for your scholars.

So here's the cardinal rule: Never hold school when public school is out! You don't want envy to flow in the wrong direction. You want those public school kids on your side, telling your kids, "You're so lucky you're homeschooled!"

As a homeschooler, you have an awesome product that leaves the competition in the dust. Present this nifty little idea in its best light to your target market. To sell your product properly, you must first create a need for it. This is traditionally pulled off by mudslinging the competition. Well, that's easy enough. Just fill in the "you're so lucky because" blank: Because you don't have to trudge uphill both ways in the blizzard to catch the school bus. Because you don't have to eat barfy cafeteria food that looks back at you from the tray. Because you don't have to be called a nerd or a geek or a brainiac and feel somehow inferior because you're so smart. Because you can go swimming on a gorgeous sunny weekday afternoon.

Now highlight for your customers all the wonderful features of the product they've purchased. This is best done on a day that hasn't derailed yet—when you can still remember all the great reasons you chose to homeschool.

Talk up all the cool stuff the public school will never offer. Point out that your kids can schedule their own days off whenever they do enough work ahead to earn them. On cold mornings, they can cozy up with a schoolbook, a blanket, and a cup of hot cocoa. They get to dig for worms or catch grasshoppers for their science projects and make cookies for their math exercises. They can have a picnic lunch in the backyard whenever they want and go swimming at the park on a weekday afternoon when other kids are still in school. The list is virtually endless.

Let's talk about snow days, for example. In Tucson, Arizona, these happen maybe once every five years or so, with gusts of up to four if we get lucky. For most five-year-old Arizonans, *snow* is part of a foreign language that must be defined out of a picture book or from a video. So are words like *galoshes, icicle, snowball,* and *sled.* If the white stuff does make an appearance, it doesn't hang around long enough to stick. An Arizona snowman is two feet tall and 50 percent mud.

The days when it snows here can't pretend to call themselves snow days. Snow moments would be a far more accurate term. By the time you've stared out the window long enough to absorb the ground-shaking truth that snow is what you're seeing fall from the sky, the flakes give way to sleet and then to rain—all within fleeting seconds before your tear-filled eyes.

Last year it snowed one day (literally), and the desert rats threw a party. My son called home from work to see if it was snowing where we were, two miles away. The DJ started playing Christmas songs on the radio (it was March). My married daughters called each other and got together to celebrate by baking cookies and lighting the fireplace, but it got too warm and they wound up opening all the windows.

If you sneeze during a snowfall here, you'll miss it entirely, which is a real shame after you've waited so long. So now you can see the great advantage of being a homeschooled kid in Tucson. Imagine seeing the snow finally fall while you're sitting locked inside a classroom doing fractions. By the time the bell rings, it's over.

And you didn't even get to build an Arizona snowman. That is *so* not fair.

Now, you must face the facts. Even after you've done your best job and pitched all the benefits with all the hype you can possibly muster, you may yet face the inevitable and dreaded "I wish I could go to public school just once."

When all else fails, send them with a friend to satisfy their curiosity. One day (or less!) of public school will cure the "yeah, buts" and they'll come home forever sold. But wait till they're old enough to know the difference.

Till then, brainwash them with the benefits.

Lifesavers

1. Is discipline really that important? God thinks so. In fact, he thinks having respectful kids is so important that he made it a requirement for positions of church leadership:

[A bishop must be] one who rules his own house well, having his children in submission with all reverence (for if a man does not know how to rule his own house, how will he take care of the church of God?); . . . Let deacons be the husbands of one wife, ruling their children and their own houses well.

1 Timothy 3:4–5, 12

189

2. If the measures for enforcing discipline in the daily schedule shock you—especially that hard-nosed one about withholding breakfast till chores have been completed—let me give you some ammunition. This will help you to settle the matter in your own heart, yes. But more than that, it will give you a scriptural answer when your kid tells you how wrong it is that you're imposing dietary sanctions on their poor little bellies:

For even when we were with you, we commanded you this: If anyone will not work, neither shall he eat. . . . But as for you, brethren, do not grow weary in doing good.

2 Thessalonians 3:10, 13

Whenever you feel you're being too tough on those kids, remember that teaching them to receive parental correction is vital to their learning to receive spiritual correction from others and directly from God himself:

Furthermore, we have had human fathers who corrected us, and we paid them respect. Shall we not much more readily be in subjection to the Father of spirits and live? For they indeed for a few days chastened us as seemed best to them, but He for our profit, that we may be partakers of His holiness. Now no chastening seems to be joyful for the present, but painful; nevertheless, afterward it yields the peaceable fruit of righteousness to those who have been trained by it.

Hebrews 12:9–11

3. Making the most of the days we have on earth by drawing up a schedule to maximize our time is also a scriptural concept. Moses prayed:

So teach us to number our days,
That we may gain a heart of wisdom.

Psalm 90:12

and the apostle Paul said,

See then that you walk circumspectly, not as fools but as wise, redeeming the time because the days are evil. Therefore do not be unwise, but understand what the will of the Lord is.

Ephesians 5:15–17

4. No matter how we've tried, the days still come when chaos tries to overtake our peace and stab it into submission. By faith in God's supernatural power over us, our circumstances, and our days, we can still triumph. Just remember:

For whatever is born of God overcomes the world. And this is the victory that has overcome the world—our faith. Who is he who overcomes the world, but he who believes that Jesus is the Son of God?

1 John 5:4–5

And the peace of God, which surpasses all understanding, will guard your hearts and minds through Christ Jesus.

Philippians 4:7

The Holdout
Factor

Pregnancy's Only Worth It
after Nine Months

How would you like half a face-lift? Or a cruise to the mid-Atlantic? How about vowing, "Till the first argument do us part"? Would you be happy with a new car that quits three blocks from the dealership? Or a bumper-to-bumper guarantee that covers nothing in between? How would you like a husband who's faithful for two weeks?

Commitment is only commitment when you make it to the finish line. If the captain of our cross-country team trained faithfully for two years and then binged on donuts and junk food the week before competition, we'd have a problem with that. Commitment is all about the long haul. If you commit to a task, you see it through come what may. All that rain, hail, sleet, and dark of night stuff makes us appreciate the postman for completing his appointed rounds.

Adversity is part of victory, but only if we don't give up.

Why do we cheer for Cinderella when she drives her pumpkin to the palace? Not because she had it all going for her, but because she didn't. Cinderella had a secret: When the going gets tough, the tough call in the fairy godmother.

But the tougher call on God the Father. Did you hear from God on your initial homeschool decision? God doesn't change his mind. But sometimes his children do. Then we feel as if we're out there all alone. But God says, "I'll never leave you or forsake you" (Heb. 13:5). If he didn't move, I wonder who did?

The fact that public education uses our kids as guinea pigs makes us mad, and we have every right to be. But are we guilty of the same offense? Are your kids simply variables in your personal homeschool experiment? Did you take up home education as a hobby? A fad? A let's-do-it-till-it-quits-being-fun thing?

Commitment means continuing what seemed exciting a long time ago even after the novelty has worn off. Homeschoolers have hit a fork in the road and chosen one path over the other. It's important to stay the course.

Planes need runways because without a long, smooth, paved surface, the plane would never get up to speed. You need also to take off at the right speed and in the right direction. But that's only part of the story. You must *maintain* air speed and heading if you expect to reach your destination. The pilot files his flight plan and doesn't redesign it at the halfway point. Not unless he wants to run out of gas.

On beyond Defrost

If you decided to homeschool, then hunker down for the long haul. There's a reason they haven't invented the five-minute school term yet. Or the two-week diploma.

Lack of patience is an occupational hazard of the microwave generation. In the olden days, people had to wait more than a punch of the defrost setting to see results. And guess what? Some things still aren't microwaveable. You still can't do a quick-cook pregnancy, and you still can't zap knowledge into a kid's brain.

Remember when you taught your children to read? Those were the glory days. "Sound out each of these letters . . . this sound says mmm, this one says ă and this one says nnn. Good! Now put them together, m—ă . . . What does that say together? m-ă . . . Say each sound slowly . . . now quickly . . ."

Then one day you sit down and voilà! He's putting whole words together one after the other! No, wait . . . now he's stringing whole sentences together! Now he's reading the newspaper! The light has gone on at last! First you cheer . . .

Then you just want to strangle him! Why couldn't he do that yesterday? Or two weeks ago? Or last month? How long have we been working on this? Yep, I sure don't miss some of those days.

But all things considered, homeschool is the farmer thing to do. The law of sowing and reaping says you must commit the time and effort up front in order to see results down the road. The farmer doesn't go out into the field and run around picking blossoms off all the plants because they're so beautiful at the moment. He knows that the withering process catches up with the pretty blossoms, but the fruit will come afterward and remain.

So it is with homeschool. It isn't always pretty and it sure takes a long time, but what you get is worth the wait, the time, and the work invested. Anything worth doing takes time—and lots of prayer. Are you praying daily for your kids and their lessons? That they'll understand? That they'll learn? That they'll get it? That you'll both survive long enough to see them get it?

Delayed answers don't indicate a lack of God's will. An answer that doesn't come immediately is still an answer. Sometimes, the answer comes immediately but isn't the one you expected. Sometimes the answer is no. But most often, the answer is *wait.*

And *wait* is definitely a four-letter word in our fax, zap, and e-mail world.

Did you seek God? Did he show you that homeschool was the right choice for you? Then take a deep breath and commit for the long haul. You'll sow in tears sometimes, but you'll reap in joy. And your kids, your first and most important disciples, will have your godly input rather than the world's agenda to base their lives upon. There is light at the end of the homeschool tunnel, but we won't reach it if we stop in the middle. Have patience and push through.

Yes, it's true that in our microwave generation anything requiring more than a minute is ashamed to be called fast food. But then again, fast food is never worth the wait.

And You Think You've Waited!

Every hero of the faith waited a whole lot longer than you have, or even longer than you ever will, over your homeschool career. Let's consider a few examples:

Abraham received the promise that he'd be the father of many nations at age seventy-five. Sarah finagled the

195

birth of Ishmael eleven years later, and fourteen years after that, Isaac the son of promise was born.

David was seventeen years old when the prophet Samuel anointed him king over all of Israel, and by the age of twenty-two and a half he reigned over one whole tribe. He had to wait another seven and a half years to reign over all of Israel as God had promised him.

Caleb waited forty years till the last whiner's skeleton bleached in the desert so that he could kill his giant and take his mountain at age eighty-five.

Joseph dreamed about the sheaves when he was just seventeen years old. Then he spent thirteen years in an Egyptian prison on trumped-up charges and was made second to the pharaoh at age thirty.

Moses was forty when he left Egypt, eighty when he returned to face Pharaoh, and one-hundred-twenty when he reached the borders of the Promised Land.

The Bible says the steps of a good man are ordered by the Lord, and the Lord holds him up while he walks so he doesn't fall (Ps. 37:23–24). Notice it doesn't say the road has no bumps. It doesn't say there are no obstacles to go around or jump over. But it does say that God chose the road for us and he'll help us make it through.

Homeschool is a lot like marriage. Once you're in, you're in for a long time. So you'd better do lots of praying up front and, once the decision is made, do whatever it takes to make it work. No back doors. No escape hatches.

"Babe! This is the happiest moment of my life! I so look forward to getting a divorce if it doesn't work out!" Is this how you responded to your husband's proposal of marriage? I don't think so.

"Hey, kids! Guess what? I'm gonna homeschool you for as long as I'm excited about it. And if it doesn't work out, we'll just throw you back in for the buzzards to pick clean!"

Calvin Coolidge said, "Nothing in the world can take the place of persistence. Talent will not. Nothing is more common than unsuccessful men with talent. Genius will not. Unrewarded genius is almost a proverb. Education will not. The world is full of educated derelicts."[1]

God often requires his people to wait, to be faithful and persist in what he's set before them. He alone is the omnipotent one who will solve the problems of the human race, including the obstacles that will face you in your homeschooling task.

Ground Crew

The most important part of homeschooling isn't curriculum or location or hours or rules. It's you. There's no substitute for you. You make up your mind, you settle the issue in your heart, and you partner with God in a great endeavor. A life-changing endeavor. A long-term endeavor. Can you do it? Of course. You can do all things through Christ, and nothing is impossible with God. That's not the question.

The question is *should* you do it, and *will* you do it if you know you should? Is this something you've heard from God to do? Then make the decision, commit to it, and hang in there. Sounds pretty simple and straightforward, doesn't it?

But how do you make *you* available 24/7, not just as Mom but Teacher? Doesn't the former role consume enough of your time without finding time to do the latter? You bet! And the most natural reaction when you feel like you're drowning is to flail around for help.

Just remember where that help comes from.

Marriage counselors know that if it weren't for good old human selfishness, they'd be out of a job. Many couples approach marriage believing their spouse exists to make them happy and to meet their every need. That's a pretty tall order for a mortal. In fact, mortals were never designed for this job description. A spouse who looks to her partner rather than to God for fulfillment, strength, and help is barking up the wrong tree.

Now if your husband comes home after a full day of work and makes dinner, changes diapers, goes grocery shopping, and does the dishes, you married a treasure. Asking him to teach the kids is kind of pushing it, don't you think? In fact, even if he doesn't do all of the above, it's still a lot to ask.

Many homeschool moms feel Dad is duty bound and called to help them homeschool the kids. Maybe this could work for the guys who are self-employed or for those who work from their homes, but few are so fortunate. If your guy works a regular job, it's a phenomenal blessing direct from the mighty hand of God for him to have enough steam left for educational input in the evenings.

Chris and I struck up a bargain: He never asked me to work a day in my life, and I rewarded him by being a miser. He helped me budget, and we made ends meet on one income, and I got to stay home and school the kids. Now, granted, this was back before a pound of bacon weighed twelve ounces and a five-pound sack of sugar weighed four, but it was still a challenge. To supplement I also baby-sat and did whatever else I could find to do at home and make money. But he'd come home and find me frazzled many days.

"I'm turning in my Mama button," I'd grouse. "I haven't gotten a thing done today!"

"Have you educated our children?" he'd ask. "Good. Then you got plenty done."

When the kids were doing algebra beyond my scope—and algebra is still beyond my scope, right where it belongs—you can bet that I employed Dad the calculus king to teach them what I didn't pretend to grasp. And he's always been the principal on call; and I always made sure he knew how much I appreciated that.

But if your superman comes home too dead to participate, and you and God are already all over it, let the poor guy breathe so he can be there to provide for you the next day. And the next. And the next. Build him up as the hero to your kids in this role as well. Be sure to point out that if he weren't working so hard all day for them, they wouldn't have a mom who could be home to teach them.

Could you keep a plane in the air without the ground crew? I don't think so. You'd better be awfully nice to them. They're the guys who are changing tires, filling up gas tanks, and replacing broken parts. You wouldn't want to fly if those people went on strike.

Not many husbands have the luxury of writing their own financial ticket so they can be there night and day to help you with the nitty-gritty aspects of homeschool. That doesn't mean you should write off all that your guy affords you in hard work, prayer, support, provision, backup, affection, and time off for good behavior!

One glaring flaw of humanity is to disregard our treasure till a moment after it's gone. Homeschooler Beth McDonough shares with us her firsthand insight into the meaning of lost treasures:

> Since becoming a widow, I've come to realize all I've taken for granted.
>
> My last two homeschool years since my spouse passed away have been lonely. I really do miss the many things my husband did. He picked up items from the grocery store on his way home from work. He vacuumed and helped fold clothes. When time was consumed in proj-

ects, field trips, and year-end reports—or when I was just burning out—he brought take-out food or treated us to dinner at a restaurant. In addition to the occasional flowers or a favorite candy bar, he'd often give my neck and shoulders a good massage when I felt tense from trying to juggle my many roles.

In the homeschool community the need is often stressed for the husband to support the wife. After nine years of homeschool, I agree wholeheartedly that the husband's support is vital, but it's just as vital that homeschool moms show their appreciation for that support.

Because of their schedules, many husbands can't be as supportive, and some are unaware that they can do little things like my husband did to help out. That's why it's important not to compare our husbands with other homeschool fathers, or hold them to the same standards.

We need to thank the Lord, who has given us our spouse as a precious gift.

Instead of focusing on the things they don't do, we should be thankful for what they do, like providing for our family financially so that we have the option to homeschool; loving our children; and being our friend. It's helpful to approach homeschooling without the expectation that our spouse can or will perform administrative duties, or teach, or clean house. If you regard these as a pleasant surprise, you'll always show your appreciation when your husband does them for you.

My husband was always more motivated to help when I showed gratitude for it. Certainly I would have liked him to do more. But I realized that because my husband was a salesman and put in long hours, he was physically and emotionally tired when he came home. He knew I worked hard all day, but I had to remember that he did too. When I honored that, he was more inclined to vacuum, or to help prepare a meal, or to try to be more sensitive to my needs.

My years of homeschooling are coming to a close, but I'd encourage those starting out to focus on the wonderful opportunity you have, not only to disciple your children in the ways of the Lord, but to nurture your marriage and to thank God for your spouse![2]

Be sure your ground crew gets lots of kudos. Inspire appreciation in your kids for everything their dad does to keep you all in the air. Don't let him be invisible and forgotten. Don't let him be perceived as a fifth wheel in the home education vehicle. He works hard to do his part of the job behind the scenes. He's the one who makes it possible for you to do your part of the job as well. He's a big part of how God is enabling the whole job to be done.

The Foolishness of God Is Wiser than Men

Maybe it's just natural cussedness. Maybe we're ahead of our time. Maybe if we know it's right, we just barrel ahead regardless of popular opinion. And as Christians, after all, we're called to that. To be the head and not the tail. To turn the battle to the gates. To not be afraid of their faces. We must strive for that and teach our kids to do the same.

But controversy for its own sake is hollow without a cause and a supportive argument. The good news is that arguments abound for God's creative design in the universe. My honors teacher, a humanistic biology professor, upheld before the entire class the creationist evidence I offered because the irrefutable laws of science were put into place by God himself.

The first and second laws of thermodynamics are universally accepted by the scientific community, creationist or not. The first law states that matter is neither created nor destroyed, proving that there was only one creation. The second law states that matter left to itself goes into

Papa Perks

Hail to the chief! Give honor where it's due.

Hugs and kisses from Mom and kids as Dad arrives home.

Stop and sit down with kids and really listen to how his day went.

Have kids help you prepare his favorite meal on a regular old day.

You and kids take off his shoes and give him a foot and neck rub.

Have kids show him special projects/papers while dinner cooks.

Kids can make a poster or story together: Why My Dad's the Best.

Surprise thank-you card or welcome banner for no particular reason.

Plan to meet him after work at the park or the library or the movies.

Have the kids present an impromptu drama or music recital for him.

Have them dress up and serve dinner by candlelight with paper menus.

Cardinal Rule: No lessons on a day when Dad's off. Be there for him.

greater decay, or entropy, proving that things don't evolve, but rather degenerate.

Mr. Biology was forced to agree that both of these accepted laws refute evolution.

There's no greater rush than standing firm for what you believe in the face of adversity and then seeing God move to back you up. As student speaker at my long-overdue college graduation, I knew I'd have the chance to glorify God in front of thousands of people, and I was excited. When the graduation committee and board of governors asked to see my speech ahead of time, I sent in a tamer version and prayed. Still, I got the inevitable phone call.

"Everybody loved your speech, but we feel that some of it may offend the student body."

"Really. Well, I've sat in classrooms for two years while the student body offended me. I've earned the right to tell them that I'm graduating because of God's grace. If the student body doesn't like that, they can get up and leave. If the board of governors doesn't like it, they can call in my alternate. But if they put me behind the lectern, I intend to glorify God."

There was a long pause.

"We don't have an alternate. You're it."

"Really. Wow. That shows an astounding lack of foresight."

"Let me call you back . . ."

The board of governors ended by telling me I could say whatever I chose, which is just as well, since I would have anyway. To everyone's surprise, the speech met with thunderous applause from the student body.

The moral of the story: If they don't agree with you, at least they'll respect you. Teach your kids this lesson. Teach them to arm themselves. Study to show yourself approved, the Bible says. Rightly divide the Word of Truth. Be the cream of the crop armed with the power of God. Daniel and his friends knew where they stood and why they stood there, and wouldn't budge for the world. That's the essence of a Christian.

When Paul stood on Mars Hill, he used his knowledge of the Jewish Bible as a Pharisee, coupled with the world's "wisdom," to preach Jesus to the leading thinkers of Athens (Acts 17:21–32). We must do the same. God uses the foolish things to confound the wise (1 Cor. 1:20–25).

We must teach our kids to make a stand and be different. Be a leader. Nobody ever followed someone who wasn't going somewhere. Standing still is just going backward in disguise.

In *The Inferno,* Dante says that the hottest places in hell are reserved for those who, in a time of moral crisis, maintain their neutrality.[3] Journalist Edward R. Murrow said, "A nation of sheep will beget a government of wolves."[4]

Teach your kids to demand credentials of the committee of they and the powers that be. And when those people throw tomatoes, make ketchup for your french fries.

My Proclamation

They said, "You'll never make it,"
And I thought that they were right;
But I kept on heading onward,
Because I hoped I might.

And they bowed their heads in wonder,
That I lacked the sense to quit;
But I held my chin up higher,
And I didn't mind a bit.

They said, "You'll never make it,"
As the problems multiplied;
But I had to make an effort,
And to know at least I tried.

I kept on going forward,
Though my spirits sometimes lagged;
I shouldered what was lightest,
And the rest I sort of dragged.

And I found, to my amazement,
At the ending of the day,
That what they said I couldn't
I had managed anyway.

It only took three little words:
"Lord, help me," and I rid
Myself of doubt; and all they said
I'd never do . . . I did![5]

Cindy O'Connor

It's Definitely Homeschool, Mom

Dave and Mariah Ford relocated from Tucson, Arizona, to answer God's call to pastor in Liverpool, England. Dissatisfied with the public schools, the Fords began homeschooling while their children were still small. Now, after many years in the trenches, Mariah shares with us here some of the great fringe benefits that home education can afford:

"If you had it to do over again, would you choose to homeschool?" Diane asked.

My older daughter Claressa shot a glance at me. She's seventeen now, and preparing to study nursing at a university in Liverpool where we pastor. My friend Diane and her husband recently joined our ranks as overseas missionaries. Unfamiliar with the foreign school system and concerned for their children's education, they chose to homeschool.

My three kids were the oldest in the crowd of fellow Americans gathered in my home that Thanksgiving Day, so I was deemed the ranking veteran homeschooler. But I doubt that gives me authority. I know it gives me gray hair and a nervous tic, but authority? Me? Maybe by default!

These years of homeschooling have certainly seen their share of difficulty. I've dealt with my own insecurities.

205

When struggles in discipline or mastering new concepts arose, and it seemed the kids just weren't getting it, it opened a can of worms for me. I'd be plagued with myriad questions: Am I a bad teacher? A bad mom? A bad wife? Can I switch hats from mom to wife to teacher without losing my mind? What about the housework? Can I really do this thing? Isn't there *anything* I can excel at?

And the major recurring question: "God, where are you?"

Of course in retrospect I see he was right there beside me, leading me every step of the way. But as one question led to another, I became a great big lump of insecurity and—yes, I have to be honest—self-pity.

My husband and I decided to homeschool our children during their elementary years in order to give them a strong foundation. We wanted them to have solid academic skills such as reading phonetically and reciting multiplication tables in their sleep. We wanted plenty of time at home to instill biblical values and truth into their young hearts and minds.

Homeschooling has been the greatest challenge of my life to date. But God is always faithful to help, and I know he didn't bring me this far to leave me.

These years at home have helped ready my children to enter into the individual destinies God has prepared for them. Knowing that her children are equipped to do the will of God is the greatest joy and comfort there is for a mother this side of heaven.

I've been challenged as wife, mom, and Christian woman beyond what I thought I could handle. But these years have been a wonderful time of growth and joy for us as a family, and for me individually. God, my loving Father, has carried me and taught me, just as a young child learning to take his first steps. He's shown me that he has all the strength and wisdom I need. He's made every resource of heaven available to me. That's the reason I'm able to teach my children how to learn.

I firmly believe that the fantastic, close, loving relationship we have with our children was made possible by the mutual investments we've made in each other's lives through homeschooling. That investment is possible because of the investment Jesus has made in our lives.

As the eyes of my oldest daughter met mine, my friend's question was answered.

"Homeschooling, Mom. Definitely homeschooling," Claressa replied without hesitation.

In that moment all my doubts faded into insignificance. What was really important became crystal clear. Our kids love God. They are bright, intelligent, already productive members of society. We've achieved our most important goals. What more could a mom ask?

"Yes, Diane," I said. "If I had it to do over again, I would choose to homeschool."[6]

You *Can* Take It with You . . . If It's Souls

We're all working right now on the legacy we'll leave behind, whether good or bad, whether intentional or unintentional. Dave and Mariah found out what's most important isn't always what's most urgent. Want to know what's more important than working a job and providing food, clothing, and shelter for your family? Providing the same for their souls. Seeing them birthed into the kingdom of God so you can all arrive there one day. Yes, we want to teach them academics. Yes, we want to teach them to develop their own personal gifts and skills. But of all the things you teach, be sure you don't ever forget to teach and preach Jesus Christ.

Because everything else is just chaff.

Psalm 78:5–7 says, "For He established a testimony in Jacob, and appointed a law in Israel, which He commanded our fathers, that they should make them known to their children; that the generation to come might know them, the children who would be born, that they may arise and declare them to their children, that they may set their hope in God, and not forget the works of God, but keep His commandments."

Along the way you'll discover what the Fords found: As you obey God and put him first in your homeschool experience, he'll pour blessings out on your relationships. People always comment about the closeness of our family. When God is given his proper place, his love reigns supreme, shed abroad in our hearts by the Holy Spirit (Rom. 5:5). His peace that passes understanding guards our hearts and minds and reigns amid the daily chaos and turmoil (Phil. 4:7). As your children grow and find gratitude for the time and effort you spent homeschooling them, investment gives way to rewards. Not the least of which is the very close friendship of a child turned loving peer.

I challenge you: Partner with God in something eternal, fulfilling, and extremely worthwhile—your kids, their souls, their future in God, the impact they'll have on their own generation, and on generations upon generations to come. You can do it.

Will you do a perfect job? Of course not. Do we ever? Homeschoolers are humans too. Not only that, we have lives. Life gets busy. School isn't your only concern. But you can't allow the urgent to displace the important.

Do your best. Be consistent. Allow yourself to make mistakes and fall, as long as you keep getting up and dusting yourself off and heading in the right direction with Jesus.

Will it work? Of course. God will honor it. The result will far exceed anything you can ask or think. Just know that he is faithful who has promised. So hang in there. God is good and he loves you and the kids even more than you love each other.

He's on your side. You're on the kids' side.

So what are you waiting for?

Lifesavers

1. Just like anything else in our Christian walk, home-schooling will bring wonderful results after we've waited so long that we've forgotten when we started. The trick is not to think about the length of the road, but instead to find joy in the journey. You're making impact academically and spiritually. The results will be, at the end of the day, a miracle of God:

> The kingdom of God is as if a man should scatter seed on the ground, and should sleep by night and rise by day, and the seed should sprout and grow, he himself knows not how. For the earth yields crops by itself: first the blade, then the head, after that the full grain in the head. But when the grain ripens, immediately he puts in his sickle, because the harvest has come.
>
> Mark 4:26–29

2. Tough times will come. But that's when we have to hunker down and trust God and stick them out. Trials wouldn't be trials if they were easy. God will give you grace to see those trials through to victory. And there's no feeling as euphoric as a job well done with your kids, because somehow, by God's grace, you all made it.

> Those who sow in tears
> Shall reap in joy.
> He who continually goes forth weeping,
> Bearing seed for sowing,
> Shall doubtless come again with rejoicing,
> Bringing his sheaves with him.
>
> Psalm 126:5–6

That you may walk worthy of the Lord, fully pleasing Him, being fruitful in every good work and increasing in the knowledge of God; strengthened with all might, according to His glorious power, for all patience and longsuffering with joy.

Colossians 1:10–11

3. Strengthen yourself and your kids for the battle that will inevitably come because you're different. Christians always have been and always will be different. But different is good, and nothing worth having comes cheap. Just remember that it's not about you, and at the end of his Book, God promises we'll come out on top. What more could we ask?

Therefore Jesus also, that He might sanctify the people with His own blood, suffered outside the gate. Therefore let us go forth to Him, outside the camp, bearing His reproach. For here we have no continuing city, but we seek the one to come.

Hebrews 13:12–14

Yes, and all who desire to live godly in Christ Jesus will suffer persecution.

2 Timothy 3:12

For this is the will of God, that by doing good you may put to silence the ignorance of foolish men.

1 Peter 2:15

And they overcame [Satan] by the blood of the Lamb and the word of their testimony, and they did not love their lives to the death.

Revelation 12:11

Conclusion

Hindsight Is Better than Foresight

Okay! We're there. We're busy. We're all pumping it and it's taking off.

But will it work?

Now there's a question over which I spent many a night biting my fingernails down to the first knuckle. As we all know, moms come off the assembly line with standard-issue eyes in the back of their heads. These permit ease of hindsight but not much foresight.

Remember me, the high school dropout trying to educate my kids at a time when homeschoolers were rebels and homeschooling was a four-letter word? I had no clue as to how I'd proceed, where I'd wind up, or whether the kids would get a decent education.

I trembled at the thought of spending twelve years getting them a high school diploma that possibly no institution of higher learning would honor.

What would become of them? Was I doing the right thing? There was no way to see the end product, and I couldn't look back because I hadn't even put the thing into gear yet. And neither had anybody else. I couldn't go to a local support group or regional rally and feel gratified to see that I wasn't the only weirdo because—confidentially—I was.

But thankfully God has a warm place in his heart for weirdos. He had called us to an off-the-wall task (his favorite kind!) and we knew he'd be there for us and for the kids. He promised to hold us up in his hands so we wouldn't stub our toes on the rocks (Psalm 91) or melt our brains on the SATs.

People look at what they perceive to be our track record and get the amusing idea that we're homeschool experts. Customarily, these aren't people who know us very well. The fact that the kids all came through and did well—the fact that I had some semblance of a brain left to go to college alongside them and get my own degree—is not a tribute to us by any stretch of the imagination. It's a tribute to God's great grace, power, and awesome love.

"Hey, Mom," said my married daughter Debbie, "a lady I met in New Orleans is going to give you a call about homeschooling."

"Poor her. Won't she be disappointed! Why do you keep giving people my number?"

"No, she won't be. She's calling you because you're a homeschool guru."

"Right. Who tells them this stuff? Do you guys put up posters, give out flyers, or what?"

"Well, somehow my husband gets it into conversations that I was homeschooled."

"Big deal! Don't you guys have anything else to talk about?"

"It *is* a big deal. Anyway, she's calling because she wants to know what you know."

"That'll take about three minutes. I'll tell her what I told your other lady from Texas."

"What did you tell her?"

"What do you think I told her? *Get on your knees!* That's all that I know."

"Tell her that. That's what she needs to hear."

It's what we all need to hear.

Every good and perfect gift comes down from above, from the Father of lights, says James (1:17), and in verse 5 he says God won't get mad if we ask him for wisdom. It's no shock to God that we don't have any. He's waiting to dish it out if we ever get smart enough to ask him for it. Then he makes us look good, and we stand in awe alongside the rest of the world at the other end.

Just use your back-of-the-head peepers and you'll see where you've been and how God's been with you every step of the way as you stuck to your guns and trusted him. Turn on those back-up lights. Everything looks better in retrospect.

But you can't look back till you've gotten down the road apiece.

Feel free to call for encouragement and prayer:

Chris and Sue Maakestad
(520) 889–8478
or e-mail: sue@maakestads.com

Helping Hands
for Homeschoolers

General Information and Support

National Home Education Network
P.O. Box 1652
Hobe Sound, FL 33475-1652
Phone: (413) 581-1463
www.nhen.org

Homeschool Support Network
P.O. Box 1056/51 West Gray Road
Gray, ME 04039
Phone: (207) 657-2800
www.homeeducator.com

A to Z Home's Cool Homeschooling
Attn: Ann Zeise
1949 Grand Teton Dr.
Milpitas, CA 95035
www.gomilpitas.com/homeschooling

Homeschool SuperSearch
Josefina R. Howard
Re: HomeschoolSuperSearch.net
PSC 451 Box 303, FPO AE 09834-3800
www.homeschoolsupersearch.net

Creation Science Organizations

Answers in Genesis
P.O. Box 6330
Florence, KY 41022
Phone: (800) 778-3390
www.answersingenesis.org

Institute for Creation Research
P.O. Box 2667
El Cajon, CA 92021
Phone: (800) 628-7640
www.icr.org

Legal Information and Support

Home School Legal Defense Association
P.O. Box 3000
Purcellville, VA 20134-9000
Phone: (540) 338-5600
www.hslda.org

Pacific Justice Institute
P.O. Box 4366
Citrus Heights, CA 95611
Phone: (916) 857-6900
www.pacificjustice.org

The Rutherford Institute
P.O. Box 7842
Charlottesville, VA 22906-7842
Phone: (804) 978-3888
www.rutherford.org

Educational Freedom.com
Attn: Donna M. DePaolo
P.O. Box 1175
Tallevast, FL 34270
www.educationalfreedom.com

Resources and Networking

Home Education Magazine
P.O. Box 1083
Tonasket, WA 98855
Phone: (800) 236-3278
www.home-ed-magazine.com

The Resourceful Homeschooler
Attn: Ricka Gerstmann
206 23rd Ave. SE
Puyallup, WA 98372
Phone: toll free (877) 523-0494
www.resourcefulhomeschooler.com

Crosswalk Homeschool
www.homeschool.crosswalk.com

The Homeschool Zone
Attn: Joe Spataro
P.O. Box 3541
Matthews, NC 28106
www.homeschoolzone.com

Homeschool Central
2337 S. Lima St.
Aurora, CO 80014
Phone: (303) 306-9323
www.homeschoolcentral.com

Practical Homeschooling Magazine
Home Life, Inc.
P.O. Box 1190
Fenton, MO 63026-1190
Phone: (800) 346-6322
www.home-school.com

Eclectic Homeschool Online
P.O. Box 50188
Sparks, NV 89435-0188
www.eho.org

Notes

Chapter 1: Light in the Black Hole

1. Woodrow Wilson, quoted on "Apple Seeds," http://www.appleseeds.org/Dec_97.htm (accessed 2 December 2003).

Chapter 2: "We Have Met the Enemy and He Is Us"

1. Albert Einstein, quoted on "Albert Einstein Quotes," 1997, http://www.sfheart.com/einstein.html (accessed 2 December 2003).

2. Ken and Bonnie Laue, interview, February 2003, used by permission.

3. Siegfried and Therese Engelmann, *Give Your Child a Superior Mind* (New York: Simon and Schuster, 1966), 61–62.

4. Terry Dorian, Ph.D., and Zan Peters Tyler, *Anyone Can Homeschool* (Lafayette, La.: Huntington House, 1996), 30.

5. Walter B. Barbre, Ph.D., *Growing Up Learning* (Washington, D.C.: Acropolis Books Ltd., 1985), 15.

6. Sam B. Peavey, Ed.D., *Observations and Perspectives on Home Education Prepared for the Iowa State Board of Education,* 5 August 1989, 2.

7. Charles J. Sykes, *Dumbing Down Our Kids: Why American Children Feel Good About Themselves But Can't Read, Write, or Add* (New York: St. Martin's Press, 1995), 190.

8. James Madison, quoted on "The Quotation Page," 2000, http://www.quotationspage.com/quotes/James_Madison (accessed December 2003).

9. National Commission on Excellence in Education, *A Nation at Risk: The Imperative for Educational Reform (An Open Letter to the American People),* 26 April 1983, 35.

10. Ibid., 15.

11. Monica Moreno, interview, March 2003, used by permission.

12. Engelmann, *Give Your Child a Superior Mind,* 14.

Chapter 3: Genius Builders Anonymous

1. Peter de Jager, "It did Happen," 2002, http://www.technobility.com/docs/futurist%2002.htm (accessed December 2003).

2. Richard W. Riley, quoted in "Riley Calls for Greater Family Involvement to Increase Learning; Announces Nationwide Partnership," *U.S. Department of Education,* 7 September 1994, http://www.ed.gov/PressReleases/09-1994/fippres.html (accessed 2 December 2003).

3. National Commission on Excellence in Education, *A Nation at Risk,* 5.

4. Ibid., 14.

5. Ibid., 8–9.

6. Ibid., 18.

7. Ibid., 24.

8. Sykes, *Dumbing Down Our Kids,* 9.

9. Charles S. Clark, "Parents and Schools," *The CQ Researcher* 5, no. 3 (20 January 1995): 51.

10. Daniel Golden, "Colleges Recruit Home-Schooled Kids," *Wall Street Journal,* 11 February 2000, 1.

11. Ibid.

12. Ibid.

13. Ibid.

14. "Famous Homeschoolers," 2000, http://www.christianhomeschoolers.com/hs/famous.shtml (accessed December 2003).

15. James C. Carper, Ph.D., "Homeschooling History and Historians: The Past as Present," *The High School Journal* (Chapel Hill, N.C.: University of North Carolina Press, 1992), 256.

16. John Wesley Taylor V, Ph.D., *Home-Based Education: An Alternative That Works* (Rapidan, Va.: Hartland Institute, 1987), 1–2.

17. Steven Mintz and Susan Kellogg, *Domestic Revolutions: A Social History of American Family Life* (New York: Free Press, 1988), xiv.

18. Tina Lewis, interview, June 2003, used by permission.

19. Engelmann, *Give Your Child a Superior Mind,* 37.

20. Ibid.

21. Peavey, *Observations and Perspectives,* 2.

22. Mark K. Smith, "Maria Montessori," *Informal Education Homepage,* 8 May 1997, http://www.infed.org/thinkers/et-mont.htm (accessed December 2003).

Chapter 4: You're So Lucky You're Homeschooled!

1. Golden, "Colleges Recruit Home-Schooled Kids," 1.

2. Dorian and Tyler, *Anyone Can Homeschool,* 29.

3. Engelmann, *Give Your Child a Superior Mind,* 79.

4. Paul Lee Tan, *Encyclopedia of 7700 Illustrations* (Rockvile, Md.: Assurance Publishers, 1979), 945.

5. Yes, the fish-and-chips Mercedes story is true. Visit Mr. Tansley at "Veg-Oil-Car.com," 2001, http://www.geocities.com/vegoilcar (accessed December 2003).

6. Steve Badaracco, personal correspondence, used by permission.

7. Sheila Hagar, "Homeschool and the Average Parent," *Oregonian,* 22 July 2001, Sunday Forum section, p. 1. Adapted and used by permission.

8. Ibid.

9. Engelmann, *Give Your Child a Superior Mind,* 27.

10. Dana Mihalko, interview, February 2003, used by permission.

11. Weldon M. Hardenbrook, *Missing from Action: Vanishing Manhood in America* (Nashville: Thomas Nelson, 1987), 38–39.

12. R. C. Sproul Jr., "Hit and Run," *Every Thought Captive,* vol. 4, issue 1, 2002, www.Gospelcom.net/hsc/ETC/Volume_Four/Issue_One/HitandRun (accessed December 2003).

13. Bill and Donna Tinsley, interview, 2 January 2003, used by permission.

14. Luci Shaw, May 2000, http://www.timothyreport.homestead.com/may2000.html (accessed December 2003).

Chapter 5: Education Is More than Academics

1. Fitzhugh Mullan, "Rx for Reading," *Los Angeles Times–Washington Post News Service* (12 March 2000).

2. Mark Twain, *The Adventures of Tom Sawyer* (New York: Aerie Books Ltd., 1983), 15.

3. R. C. Sproul Jr., "So Be True to Your School: The School House," *Every Thought Captive,* vol. 2, issue 4, 1998, www.gospelcom.net/hsc/ETC/Volume_Two/Issue_Four/The_School_House (accessed December 2003).

4. *The New Strong's Complete Dictionary of Bible Words* (Nashville: Thomas Nelson, 1996), 107, 1, 244, 73, 175, 26, 11, 222, 141.

5. Tina Lewis, interview, May 2003, used by permission.

6. Sykes, *Dumbing Down Our Kids,* 52

7. Ibid., 114.

8. Charles J. Sykes, "Fourteen Rules Kids Won't Learn In School," e-mail message to the author, 4 December 2003, used by permission.

9. Albert Einstein, quoted on "Albert Einstein Quotes," 1997, http://www.sfheart.com/einstein.html (accessed 2 December 2003).

10. John McCain, with Mark Salter, *Faith of My Fathers: A Family Memoir* (New York: Random House, 1999), 335–36.

11. Ibid., 322.

12. Ibid., 331.

13. Cited in Sykes, *Dumbing Down Our Kids,* 138.

14. Ibid., 138.

15. Ibid., 56.

16. Jim Hightower, *There's Nothing in the Middle of the Road but Yellow Stripes and Dead Armadillos: A Work of Political Subversion* (New York: HarperCollins, 1998).

Chapter 6: A Function of Dysfunction

1. Adapted from "Being Wealthy," March 2003, http://www.all-creatures. org/stories/beingwealthy.html (accessed December 2003).

2. Josh McDowell, *Beyond Belief to Convictions* (Carol Stream, Ill.: Tyndale, 2002), 5.

3. Steve Badaracco, interview, 12 February 2003, used by permission.

4. "Left Coast Hall of Shame," *National Liberty Journal,* March 2003, http://www.nljonline.com/march03/left_coast.htm (accessed December 2003).

Chapter 7: The House You Have with You Always

1. Donna Cohn, interview, September 1998, used by permission.

2. Engelmann, *Give Your Child a Superior Mind,* 51.

3. Carolyn Schlicher, personal correspondence, November 2002, used by permission.

4. Keith Geiger, "President's Viewpoint," *NEA Today* (April 1994): 2.

Chapter 9: The Holdout Factor

1. Calvin Coolidge, quoted on "The Quotation Page," 1994, http://www. quotationspages.com/quotes/Calvin_Coolidge (accessed December 2003).

2. Beth McDonough, personal correspondence, January 2003, used by permission.

3. Dante Alighieri, *La Comedia Divina,* trans. Geoffrey L. Bickersteth, "Inferno," canto 3, lines 35–42 (1972).

4. Edward R. Murrow, quoted on "Quotations to Remember," November 1997, http://www.tameri.com/csw/quotes.html#Politics (accessed 3 December 2003).

5. Cindy O'Connor, "My Proclamation," 2001, http://oconnor6.tripod.com/ poem12.html (accessed December 2003). Used by permission.

6. Mariah Ford, personal correspondence, October 2002, used by permission.

Sue Maakestad and her husband, Chris, have been married for thirty-one years. For twenty-four of those years they homeschooled their eight children from birth through high school. The youngest, age nineteen, recently received his computer software degree. The rest are gainfully employed and/or married college graduates. Sue speaks for homeschool conventions on request and was a featured speaker for the Spring 2003 Bay Area Convention of CHEA (Christian Home Education Association). She is a contributing author for the marriage anthology *One True Vow* (Barbour, 2001) and has written for *Home Education Magazine* and the *Arizona Families for Home Education Journal*. The Maakestads also edit *Bull's Eye,* a quarterly Christian parenting publication sponsored by The Door Christian Fellowship, their Tucson, Arizona, church home of twenty years.